KAYAK SURFING

bill mattos

www.pesdapress.com

First published in Great Britain 2004 by Pesda Press
'Elidir', Ffordd Llanllechid
Rachub, Bangor
Gwynedd
LL57 3EE

Design & artwork info@magicdot.co.uk
Printed by Cambrian Printers - Wales
Copyright © 2004 Bill Mattos

ISBN 0-9547061-0-2

Having spent over three months rowing solo across the Atlantic in a small plywood boat I was hooked, not only by the immense beauty of the ocean, but on the elation of surfing thirty foot waves.

On returning to the UK I was desperate to be at one with the ocean again, feeding off its energy. Kayak surfing seemed the obvious solution. The problem was that kayaking had moved on a great deal during my five year break from the sport. I felt completely out of touch.

foreword
Debra Veal, MBE

I was totally frustrated by the lack of good material out there. I had always thought of kayaking as a cool sport and there's certainly no doubting the coolness of board surfing, so it was a mystery to me that previous aqua authors had managed to make kayak surfing look so uncool.

Bill Mattos has proved, through his words and pictures, just how sexy kayak surfing can be. He has an amazing ability to paint a picture with words.

The dry nature of instructional books has been avoided through good humour and inspirational photography. But to pigeon-hole it as an instructional book alone would be wrong. Go on... take a peek. You will not be disappointed.

KAYAK SURFING

bill mattos

contents

This is not a book of rules...

In a sense surfing is all about creativity. But it's difficult to be creative while sticking to a set of rules. The rules are there to stop you from being unpopular with people who have fixed ideas about everything in general, and surfing in particular, not to stop you from experimenting.

ARRANGED SEQUENTIALLY

to surf, or not to surf? _____ 8
what is surfing? _____ 13
what you'll need _____ 14
where to start _____ 18
getting there _____ 22
taking off _____ 26
ride direction _____ 28
simple turns _____ 30
weight shift _____ 32
controlling speed _____ 34
ten commandments _____ 36
core moves _____ 51
bottom turn _____ 52
top turn _____ 54
radical top turn _____ 58
cutback _____ 60
radical cutback _____ 62
slides _____ 64
rebounds _____ 66
exiting _____ 68
core info _____ 72
the crystal ball _____ 73
making it _____ 79
race ahead _____ 80
carve around _____ 82
tuck under _____ 86
floater _____ 88
workin' it _____ 91
it's your call _____ 92
think... _____ 95

surviving _____ 97
rip till you die _____ 100
the purpose of moves & tricks _____ 106
radical moves _____ 109
snap _____ 110
slash _____ 112
layback _____ 113
spin _____ 114
tube ride _____ 118
aerial _____ 122
paddle out tricks _____ 124
blunt & barrel roll _____ 128
chi _____ 130
charc _____ 132
training & fitness _____ 135
training for surf kayaking _____ 138
preparation _____ 140
competition _____ 142
serious performance gear _____ 145
boats _____ 146
gear & clothing _____ 148
fin & paddles _____ 150
epilogue _____ 155
glossary _____ 156
acknowledgements _____ 158
suggested reading _____ 159

This book is intended to fit snugly in the hand, the bag, or the glove compartment, and, if you believe in Zen, to fall open easily at the very page you should probably be reading today. Obviously, it may not get this right every time, but what do you expect?
...It's only a book after all!

Bill Mattos

PLATES

Tahiti - French Polynesia
Bill Mattos charging on a super-shallow reef. _____ 4-5

Greenaway - Cornwall - UK
Bill Mattos takes the drop on a wedging left. _____ 10-11

Havae Iti - Tahiti - Fr. Polynesia
Caught inside, Nathan Eades jumps for his life. _____ 24-25

Tahiti - French Polynesia
Hanging on a wedging right bowl. _____ 40-41

Greenaway - Cornwall - UK
Bill Mattos turns onto a glassy green wall. _____ 48-49

Polzeath - Cornwall - UK
Snap cutback. _____ 56-57

Teahupo'o - Tahiti - Fr. Polynesia
Fully committed bottom turn from Nathan Eades. _____ 70-71

Cornwall - UK
We're not sure where, but beautiful, isn't it? _____ 76-77

Polzeath - Cornwall - UK
Bill Mattos carves around the foam-ball. _____ 84-85

Teahupo'o - Tahiti - Fr. Polynesia
Steve Childs escapes by the smallest of margins. _____ 102-103

Polzeath - Cornwall - UK
Bill Mattos does a wavewheel. _____ 104-105

Scarborough - South Africa
Barrelling madness from Nathan Eades _____ 120-121

Teahupo'o - Tahiti - Fr. Polynesia
Local wave warriors. _____ 136-137

Somewhere in Tahiti
Bill Mattos, eyes on the prize. _____ 152-153

Teahupo'o - Tahiti - Fr. Polynesia
Unbelievable speed from Nathan Eades. _____ 156-157

Teahupo'o - Tahiti - Fr. Polynesia
The 'Jurassic Park' view from Teahupo'o _____ 158-159

to surf, or not to surf

that is the question

Whether 'tis nobler in the mind to stand, is hardly the point. Some of us are kayakers, and as such driven by the desire to see what dizzy heights our chosen craft can reach upon the ocean wave, without recourse to taking up a completely different sport.

Waterman n. a person with total mastery of all oceanic endeavours, the revered waterman can fish, dive, surf, windsurf, kayak, bodysurf, interpret complex weather data, and save the odd drowning man. Athletic, confident yet typically soft-spoken (choosing to let his actions do the talking), the waterman fears neither tempest nor shark and seeks not higher ground come hell or high water. He can survive entirely on self-harvested ocean bounty, catching his food from the very seas he'll surf over when the swell is up.

(adapted from surfzone.com's a-z of surfing)

I cannot guess what inspired you to pick up this book, but I can hint at what made me write it. While it is neither comprehensive nor complete, this book contains key knowledge to enable kayakers to excel in the surf. I have written it based not just on my own thirty years of kayak surfing experience, but also that of many wonderful surfers of all kinds that it has been my privilege to meet all over the world. It is not, perhaps, the right book for beginners, but perhaps it is the right place to begin. And if you enjoy it half as much as I have, then I've enjoyed it twice as much as you...

Whether by aspiring to waterman status you find yourself in need of guidance in the art of kayak surfing, or whether you are an expert kayaker who has found the surf a difficult place in which to exhibit your mastery of your chosen craft, fear not... For enlightenment lies within these very pages. Read and read again. Even he or she who has nothing to learn from such a work may find the photos, quotations and comments inspiring, thought provoking, and in some cases amusing. I hope so, anyway...

WHAT IS SURFING?   what is surfing?

what is surfing?

Well, it is riding waves, of course, as most people are well aware. The first people to do it were Polynesians in outrigger canoes, a point I'm always happy to make when surfers insist that board-riding is the only original, cool and indeed acceptable way to enjoy the waves. Which, unfortunately, happens quite a lot. Because board-riding is very cool, and so a lot of people want to be associated with it.

One thing we all learn very quickly is that good surfers (whatever their craft), appreciate any kind of water fun, and are not usually exclusive or territorial about it other than in exceptional circumstances. It's not about what you ride, it's about how you ride.

A lot of people go to crowded beach breaks and ride the broken waves, which can be exhilarating and lots of fun. In the 'soup', as it's called, you can only really ride straight towards the shore, and this means that lots of people can get on one wave. Which is fine, and fun, but it does tend to reinforce two habits that are hard to shake off. One is that of riding straight down the wave. The other is that of riding a wave with other people. Both of those habits are regarded as anti-social, if not dangerous, when you venture a little further out where the waves are steep and green.

In this book I will try to explain some things that most kayakers don't find it easy to understand. How to do exciting things in a kayak on a wave - but at the same time - how to ride in a way that is both safe and sociable for other people. I will cover all of these points in exhaustive detail later on. For now, let's take a look at some shots of different people riding different things, and try to decide where we fit into the surfing world picture.

what you'll need

apart from the desire to shred ocean waves

You're going to need a boat and a paddle. You may also need a spraydeck (sprayskirt), buoyancy aid (personal flotation device), helmet and a wetsuit and/or other stuff to keep you warm. What you really need is a kayak shop/outfitter. They will give you the best advice about the latest toys. What follows here is the basic knowledge you'll need to avoid becoming bewildered by the choices.

Safety first: Many people surf wearing a buoyancy aid, helmet and wetsuit. Many more surf with no personal protective equipment whatsoever. Attitude, environment and personal circumstances have so much bearing on this decision that it is impossible to give any advice except this – if in doubt, wear all the protective equipment imaginable.

On a sandy beach bare feet are fine. However there are many situations in which footwear is essential (see p149).

Paddle type does not make as much difference to surf kayakers as it does to other paddlers. Bear in mind though that the paddles most beginners use are rather long for surfing. Expert surf kayakers and wave skiers use paddles less than 2m (6') in length.

General purpose kayaks; sit on tops; wave skis; white water creek and freestyle boats; they all surf, and they all excel in their own areas. Most of the material in this book features high-performance surf kayaks, because they do it all. But they aren't the only suitable craft. Here's an at-a-glance overview of the different types of boat you'd most likely consider, and reasons why you should or shouldn't!

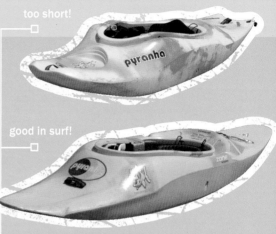

too short!

good in surf!

GENERAL PURPOSE KAYAKS

Widely available and cheap plastic boats. Usually fast and easy to paddle out through small beach-breaks. You need a spraydeck to stop the kayak filling with water, which means that you need to be able to roll, because if you fall out it will fill up and become a lethal projectile weighing over half a ton! If the boat has a flat bottom it will probably surf very well. If it's rounded it will be difficult to do a great deal with, but fine for learning in.

PLAYBOATS

Low volume, sharp rails, and rakish lines - these extreme examples of the kayak genre look as though they'd rip in the surf. But be careful. The early flat-bottomed freestylers (late '90s) are great. Some later ones have features called rocker-breaks that make them very slow and bouncy. Later still, the boats started to get really short. Sub 2.2m playboats won't really cut the mustard in the surf.

SIT-ON-TOPS

Can't fill with water, stable and inexpensive. Usually made from plastic or foam. Low in performance but high in fun factor. An ideal first kayak or something for all the family. You don't need any kayaking skills to enjoy one of these boats, but you must have a leash so that it doesn't get away and hurt someone if you fall off it!

SHORT SURF KAYAKS ⬜

Often called high-performance boats, this name derives from a competition category in which they are commonly used. Usually about 2.3m (8'6") long and made from hi-tech composites, they feature brutal rails, fins, and are characterised by a short tail. The high performance boat represents the cutting edge of surf kayaking - in the hands of an expert kayaker it can deliver rides to match those of stand-up surfers. The trade-off is that it is expensive and not particularly easy to paddle.

⬜ WAVE SKIS

A variety of extreme sit-on-top. With the same advantage - you don't need to be able to roll, you can get off. But that's where the similarity ends. Unstable and expensive, but very high performance. Hard and pointy fibreglass with sharp fins, they aren't good to hit people with.

⬜ LONG SURF KAYAKS

Designed for competition, often called International Class boats they are 3.5m (11'6") long, fast, hard-carving surf machines. They don't usually have fins due to competition regulations. They are a joy to paddle and to watch, but they are often relatively fragile due to lightweight construction in hi-tech composites.

CREEK BOATS

A disaster area in the surf. Short, round, slow and heavy plastic boats lacking well-defined rails. Their enormous volume, an advantage in descending rapids, just makes them difficult to paddle out and impossible to control on a broken wave.

where to start
tedious maths and physics, but you need to know it...

When waves approach shallow water at the shore, their lower reaches begin to drag across the ocean floor, and friction slows them down. The wave energy below the surface is directed upward, causing the waves to increase in height. The longer the swell period, the more energy there is in the wave – there is a greater volume of water elevated (and depressed) by the swell. This means that long-period waves will grow much more than short-period waves. A three-foot swell with a ten second period may only grow to be a four-foot breaking wave, while a three-foot swell with a twenty second period can grow to be a fifteen-foot breaking wave (more than five times its deep-water height, depending on the ocean floor bathymetry). As the waves pass into shallower

water, they become steeper and unstable as more and more energy is pushed upward, to a point where the waves break in water of depths about 1.3 times the swell height.

Particle motion within the wave is slowed by friction with many things. In deep water the waves will travel across the ocean almost undiminished by distance, but slow as they reach the shallower regions. The wave may arrive perpendicular to shallow water, but it may not be so. The shallows it reaches may slow one part of the wave more than another, causing sometimes unexpected changes in wave direction. The photos on the following pages show some of the ways in which waves can behave as they sweep into the surf zone.

A B

THE MEASURING OF WAVES:

For consistency most people describe wave heights by the face of the wave. We often also compare waves to a stand-up surfer's height. Assuming a surfer averages five feet tall when crouching and surfing a wave:

ONE FOOT = ANKLE HIGH

TWO FEET = KNEE HIGH

THREE FEET = WAIST HIGH

FOUR FEET = CHEST HIGH

FIVE FEET = HEAD HIGH

SIX FEET = ONE FOOT OVERHEAD

TEN FEET = DOUBLE OVERHEAD

FIFTEEN FEET = TRIPLE OVERHEAD

Hawaiians, among others, measure the back of the wave and estimate the wave back to be one half of the wave face height. Their intent is probably consistency with the deep-water swell height. But it's inherently flawed because numerous variables like swell period, diffraction and shoaling can greatly alter the transition of swell to breaking waves. In its favour, the back height is probably a better reflection of a wave's power than its height just before it breaks, but that really isn't the whole story because seabed topography can have widely differing effects on the wave's power delivery.

→

E

◄The particle motion in a wave is not in the direction it appears to be. Before the wave breaks the motion is entirely upwards at the face and downwards at the back (see the taking off page) or anticlockwise in this example. When the wave breaks, part of the water breaks away and starts to fall down the face, but the majority of the motion is still in the opposite direction. The more water that breaks away, the heavier the wave is said to be. This one is pretty heavy as waves go...

F

A Some reef breaks are super-shallow. This spot is half a mile offshore and ten foot waves are breaking. Though the wave might initially break into quite deep water, inside it is less than knee deep.

B A ridiculously heavy wave but quite slow and not that steep. This wave doesn't afford very dynamic riding yet it's extremely powerful when it breaks.

C Beach-breaks aren't always soft - this one is hollow and heavy, but at least the water is fairly deep or the bottom sandy - you can see this from the moderate splash-up as the lip rebounds. Beware breaks that splash-up higher than the wave itself, they're scary!

D An extreme reef break with a thick green lip throwing high and hard.

E Notice how this wave-front does not sweep in parallel to the shore but is distorted by the varying depth of water across the beach - a common scenario with a shifting sand bottom.

F A less throwy reef break, but still pretty extreme - this wave bowls inward leaving nowhere to run.

G An onshore wind will obliterate any steepness and turn the surf zone into a mess of whitewash with few rideable shoulders. It will also be difficult to paddle out over the waves.

H Prior inspection can reveal useful patterns and features not obvious when afloat.

I An offshore wind makes the waves hollow with spectacular spindrift, and will in time help to tidy up the swell. A strong offshore can make it hard to take off and you can be blown away by the updraft!

J A well lined up swell providing consistent, progressive rides, but fairly soft because of a gently sloping sandy bottom.

Before you can ride any waves, you need to paddle to where they are breaking. Obvious, really, but it had to be said. Few things in this life make less sense than trying to bludgeon your way through breaking surf if there is some way to paddle around to the take-off zone, but if there is no such easy option, you are going to have to put your head down and charge through the waves. Depending on your type of craft, you will find that there are different ways to make this task as painless as possible, but there are a few simple tricks that work for most situations.

TRICK Nº1 Look before you leap - **If you stand on the shore and watch for a while, you may notice consistent soft spots where the waves don't break, or don't break really hard. These may coincide with rip currents that can speed your journey out the back.**

TRICK Nº2 Use points of reference on shore - **If you can see where you want to paddle out, especially if it's a more complicated route ('halfway out I'll move 50m left') then it helps to have landmarks on the shore. An hour spent trudging (or driving) around taking note of fixed points that line up with your chosen path through the waves will probably save you at least that much time in the water.**

TRICK Nº3 Use points of reference from the water - **As you paddle out, and every time you get off a wave, take note of any landmarks that fix your position, either on land or on the seabed if you can see it. You will very quickly build up a mental picture that helps you to be in the right place at the right time.**

TRICK Nº4 Paddling straight through - **It's always tough if the waves are bigger than about 2', but sometimes it just has to be done. Kayaks can paddle over (or under) very big waves but it is fraught with difficulty and genuine physical danger, both to the kayaker and to anyone paddling out behind him should he mess it up and get hurled shorewards again. Avoid paddling through breaking waves if you can. If you can't, use one of the following techniques.**

HOW BIG IS TOO BIG? - I have seen kayakers make it through 12' breaking waves, but it calls for a big helping of skill and strength with a healthy drop of luck. And it's dangerous, especially in shallow water or crowded conditions. Each paddler has their own limits, but anything over a 4' swell is likely to have enough energy to be genuinely challenging. Beginners probably shouldn't go out if it's over 2'.

JUMPING WAVES - If at all possible, we're going over the wave. You need all the forward momentum you can muster, which means paddling at the wave full tilt. Surprisingly, most kayaks reach maximum speed in only four strokes (less for very short, slow boats, and more for long, fast ones). Don't wear yourself out before you get to the wave.
If the wave is green you'll just go right up over it. If the top is just starting to pitch, you'll be fine too, but keep your head down and make sure you don't catch a paddle blade in the lip, or you could be flipped back down the face. If the lip is throwing forward hard, you'll have to duck under it, tucking forward and keeping your paddle low and along the boat. Aim to go through the top part of the wave before you are sucked up and over the falls!

If the wave is already broken, flick the nose of your boat up at the last moment using a forward sweep and lean to the same side. The combined closing speed of your boat and the white water is considerable, and if most of it can be made to hit the hull rather than the deck, it will be converted into a vertical hop up on top of the wave. Beware the turbulence of the pile, since you'll have to keep paddling through it.

DUCKING OR PUNCHING - If experience tells you that jumping the wave isn't going to work, because it's too big or because your timing was off and you got to it just as it broke hard, you might still be able to punch straight through. Again, head down and paddle pointed along the boat. Try to hit the wave hard but present the least possible resistance to its passage. In some small boats you can even try to bounce the nose down like a duck-dive, to avoid as much as possible of the moving water.

Don't attempt to jump or punch a tubing section. The falling water will slam your nose down and as it rebounds you'll be sucked over the falls. Or, in extreme cases you'll front loop straight into the reef! And whichever combination of methods you choose, try to minimize the time you expose yourself and others to danger in the impact zone. Get through the waves to the take-off zone as quickly as you can, and start having some fun.

■ With a duck-dive the surfer can avoid the worst of it. The kayaker, however, can take advantage of greater manoeuvrability when paddling to get around, up and over the lip (see getting there, page 22).

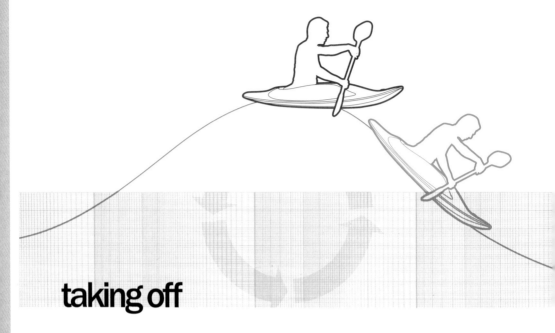

taking off

Few things demonstrate a kayaker's mettle better than how they take a wave. Many have a low success rate, expending a lot of energy paddling for take-offs but mostly letting the wave roll away unridden. Some catch the wave eventually, after much paddling. Some catch the wave too early, and have a low energy ride meandering around looking for the sweet spot.

Basically you're looking to cruise into position (without jumping the queue), turn and take just a few strokes to accelerate into a ride. You should be in the power-pocket of a breaking section right from the outset. If you do anything other than this you will either have an ugly start

to your ride that is difficult to overcome, or else you run the risk of being dropped in on because you're not playing the game in the accepted way (see the Ten Commandments p36).

Only experience can tell you how steep a wave needs to be for you to catch it with your chosen craft. But it's safe to say that unless the wave is peaking, it's not a goer in any really surf-orientated machine (maybe in a sea kayak) and that once the lip is throwing forward, it's definitely too late! So the window of opportunity is somewhere in-between. You should aim to attain wave speed before you are halfway up the wave (see the diagram above).

OBSERVATION, EXPERIENCE & SMOOTH POWER DELIVERY

are the key elements to a successful take-off

■ **LOOKING AT THE DIAGRAM -** because the motion of the water is circular as shown, it follows that once you are halfway up the face the water is trying to move you backwards and slow your take-off. Also, in small to medium sized waves, your tail will be in the back of the wave. Having the water pull your tail down presents much more drag than having it lifted up as it would be if you were low in the wave.

■ **PUTTING THE POWER IN -** practise accelerating on flat water. Be smooth, paddle only as hard as you can do without splashing or wobbling. You should be up to speed in about four increasingly long strokes. Then take it to the wave. With the help of gravity, you should get to maximum speed more easily. Take slightly longer strokes than you did on the flat. You'll be able to pull them through quicker without splashing and flailing too.

Consequently you shouldn't need more than three strokes to take off, especially if you cruised into the take-off position carrying some speed.

Whatever you do, don't wobble the boat. Following these recommendations will give you an effortless take-off, but a lot of the effortlessness comes from dynamic lift under your tail. Any wobbles will 'spill' the lift and spoil your smooth getaway.

ride direction

This is a matter the importance of which cannot be overstated. No, really. Since you are going to ride across the face of the breaking wave, it's muchos importante that you decide from the outset which way you are going to go - left or right. And this is something that most kayakers seem to have a lot of trouble with.

Most surfers will know which way they are going to go before they even take off. In some cases, you'll be paddling for a wave right on the peak or A-frame, and you'll be in a position to decide after you've taken the drop. But it's still better to decide sooner than later. Once you are at the bottom of the face with no clear direction, it is very difficult to inject any real energy into your ride.

Making this decision takes some experience, and older, wiser surfers are better at it. But the basic principles are easy to acquire – you just have to look at the wave and decide. Is the wave closer to breaking (steeper, higher, or even pitching already) at one end than at the other? You will always choose to ride from the former towards the latter. It should be pretty clear in these pictures: 01 02 03

Once you have decided which way to go, you have the option of a straight take-off, or one which is already angled the way you want to go. The latter is often a good idea. Sometimes you are a bit too deep in the section and don't want to be overtaken by the break before you get going. Or you may find that it is easier to make a smooth take-off if the boat is slightly angled to the wave face, because the shape of the wave dictates it. This tends to occur on fast, critical or barrelling waves.

In certain cases you will find that it is a good idea to take off towards the breaking section of the wave, then turn away once you are planing. This is called a fading take-off. It is useful when you are not really deep enough, and you want to get to a steeper part of the face to help your take-off.

It is also used by some experts in critical, bowl-shaped reef-breaks, because the wave wraps around so that the take off position faces the break but can go from too flat to too steep in a couple of seconds. An example of this is shown below. 04

04

To ride, you will need to be able to steer as soon as you are planing. Steering a boat that's travelling at high speed on a wave is a little different; so read on to find out how you can deal with that.

simple turns

To control your boat you'll need to be able to steer, and this is done using a combination of boat, paddle and body language - usually in about equal measure. Although you should note from the outset that the paddle is, if anything, the least part of the equation.

Surfing is all about speed, and there is no sense giving up your hard-won speed by doing anything that will slow the boat down. Which would include leaning the boat so much that it stalls, or jamming the paddle or any part of your anatomy into the water to lever a turn!

Having got up and planing, you should try to keep the boat's hull speed as high as possible, maintaining the optimum dynamic position on the wave using turns to control your velocity along the wave, rather than by varying the actual speed of the boat.

Whatever type of kayak you surf, it will have a natural tendency to turn following the shape of one or more rails on the hull. Generally speaking the more you lean the more it will turn, up to a point where the sides of the boat enter the water and start to cause a lot of drag. But often the boat will need just a little encouragement with the paddle to make it start to turn, and get the water flowing smoothly along the curves on the hull.

So lean gently and smoothly in the direction you want to turn, using your paddle in a kind of low brace position to support your weight (or just give you a bit of confidence) and pressuring the low brace blade slightly away from the boat. If necessary let the drive face of the blade be a little bit rotated to face you so that you can push away a little with the back face, but remember – this isn't a stern rudder.

Notice the low brace position with the wrists above the paddle shaft in **01** & **02**; here the non-drive face of the blade is reacting to give a 'push'. In **03** the high brace position, with the wrist below the paddle shaft, the drive face of the blade is engaged and provides a 'pull'. In all three instances the paddle is employed to provide a balancing force, not a 'turning stroke'.

NOTE ■ Any attempt to use a stern rudder at high speed will cause the water blade to act as a wing (the Bernoulli effect) and drag it away. This will a) be the opposite of the normal low-speed effect of a stern rudder, and b) if you resist the blade's attempts to move away from the hull and try to force it to work as a proper stern rudder, you will cause a ton of drag and slow the boat down. So don't use stern rudders when surfing.

Many kayakers try to use sweep strokes to turn the boat – this is also ineffective at speed. A forward sweep stroke cannot be performed with enough speed for the rate the water goes by, and if it seems to work at all, it is usually that the paddler rotated aggressively to do the stroke, which turned the boat a little. Unfortunately, when you finish the stroke and rotate back again, you undo all the good work!

That's why you often see people doing multiple sweeps without getting a solid direction change for their trouble. Reverse sweeps while surfing, obviously, slow the boat down big-time. Why would you want to do that?

You will usually find that the turn becomes more and more aggressive the longer you let it continue. At the extreme, your boat will spin out, sooner rather than later if it doesn't have fins. So just as in a car or on a bicycle you must return the steering to the centre position when (or just before) you think you have turned enough. This means getting your weight off your paddle blade and centred over the boat. Remember to do everything smoothly. Wobbles spill the lift from under the hull, and slosh water across the decks. Both of these things slow you down in a planing scenario.

Using your body weight to alter your roll, pitch and yaw is a fundamental part of dynamic kayaking. I've realised two things from writing that sentence. One is that I am going to need to explain roll, pitch and yaw. The other is that a lot of kayakers are quite wrong in their assumption about how to achieve boat language using body language.

Roll is not only the word for the way we kayakers right ourselves after a capsize. It is also the word for any rotation of the boat in that direction. If you tip the boat a little bit (say 10°) to the right, we call that 10° of right roll. Being upside down is 180° of roll.

Pitch is rotation fore and aft, me hearties. If you slowly lean as far back as you can, the nose of the boat will probably tip up a bit. Or you might fall off the back of your chair. Depends where you are.

Yaw is left and right rotation, like steering. If you are in your boat on flat water, and you rotate your body to the left, you may find that your boat turns a little the opposite way.

weight shift

Now, the thing is - most people instinctively assume that if they lean forward the boat's nose will drop, and if they move their body to the left, the boat will roll to the left. It will, but only as it rebounds from its initial reaction which happens to be the opposite. If you don't see why that makes sense, think about rolling. If you roll up from a capsize using your right paddle blade, you are rotating the boat to your left. You move your body as far to the left (towards the surface) as you can, but you actually rotate the hull by throwing your body to the right. It's that movement that is usually called a hip-flick or hip-snap.

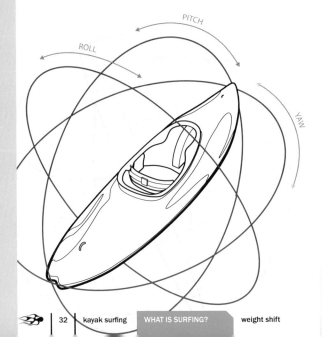

PITCH

ROLL

YAW

Newton's Third Law:
"To every action there is always
opposed an equal reaction;
or, the mutual actions of two
bodies upon each other are
always equal and directed
to contrary parts."

READ THIS CAREFULLY:

■ Leaning forward pulls the bow upward, unless you do it very slowly.

■ Leaning quickly to the left drops your right-hand rail into the water, not the left one.

I suggest trying to combine this thinking with the well-known kayaking dichotomy of edge versus lean. Edging is tipping the boat over a bit while keeping your body upright. Leaning is tipping your body over at the same angle as the boat. These two ideas are enough for a white water boater, but in the high-speed planing world of the surf we do need to have a feel for the dynamic issues as well as these static ones.

So, if you want to get your weight onto the left rail, you can do it by a quick body shift to the right, or by slowly moving over to the left and then bringing the boat after

you. Depending on how much time you have, and how long you want to keep the pressure on that left rail. See? Then bolt the edge/lean concept on as well.

Trying to stop the bow purling by leaning back is a mistake I see all too often, too. It's understandable, but you have to try to programme yourself not to do it, in the same way that you learned not to reflex-balance when you first mastered paddling a kayak (reflex balancing is the novice manoeuvre of trying to prevent a capsize to the right by leaning to the left which, as we all know, will just make matters worse).

There is also a belief that you can make the boat faster or slower by leaning forward or back. Perhaps you can a little, but it's complex and varies according to boat design. What you must remember, (mentioned elsewhere), is that the downforce of your stern in the wave is so great that the small amount of weight shift you can achieve makes very little difference. Have you ever wondered how a board surfer can ride on the very nose of his board without the board flipping up? That is the power of trailing edge downforce. We boaters can move our centre of gravity over a total range of about a foot (30cm). Not much, then.

controlling speed

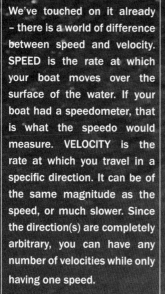

We've touched on it already – there is a world of difference between speed and velocity. SPEED is the rate at which your boat moves over the surface of the water. If your boat had a speedometer, that is what the speedo would measure. VELOCITY is the rate at which you travel in a specific direction. It can be of the same magnitude as the speed, or much slower. Since the direction(s) are completely arbitrary, you can have any number of velocities while only having one speed.

Here's an example. If you take off on a wave at point A, and ride across it until it closes out at point B, your velocity towards the beach will be the same as the speed of the wave. Usually about 10mph. Not very exciting really. But your velocity across the beach will have been more like 20mph. Your hull speed may have been over 25mph, and you probably had to make several cutbacks to make sure you stayed in the critical part of the wave.

It's is all about maintaining speed while remaining in the most dynamic part of the wave. This can be done by means of cutbacks; climbing and dropping to increase the distance travelled; and in extreme cases using a roundhouse cutback to turn back to the pocket and then regain your original ride direction. A bit like a dog

running round and round a slowcoach owner who refuses to keep up.

Every now and then, the slowcoach dog-walker (or wave) decides to put on a spurt of speed. You have to anticipate this. You can recognize a section like this because the wave will wall up steeply a long way ahead of you. Make sure you are high on the wave when it happens, ready to make use of your gravitational potential and the steepness of the section to outrun the wave. You must also anticipate the slow-down, so that you don't over-run the pocket and end up wallowing in an uncritical part of the wave. Before the section slows, indicated by a drop off in wave-height and/or steepness ahead of you, you must already be making a turn to keep yourself in the critical part of the wave.

SPEED BUMPS AHEAD

■ In critical or powerful waves you cannot always rely on being able to read the wave and react to it. This is where prior observation of the waves and other people's rides will pay dividends, perhaps saving you from reef-rash or a good kicking!

ten commandments

01 | choose your surf zone wisely

Be realistic about your ability, and your goals. You need to accept that some surf zones are suited to learning skills, some to aggressive surfing, rarely both.

Surf spots with hollow, powerful, high performance waves (and I don't just mean Teahupo'o, Mavericks and Pipeline – there are critical breaks a lot less extreme than these famous ones) suit a skilled and competitive type of surfer. Generally at such breaks, the better you are the more waves you will ride.

At the other end of the spectrum there are less critical waves like my local break of Polzeath in Cornwall. These soft breaks usually feature lots of beginners or intermediate surfers. The line-up will be considerably more relaxed, with much less pressure on the individual to rip it up.

In between there are a variety of spots, many of which aren't particularly critical or soft, but may well vary according to a given day's waves or population.

When it comes to deciding where you are going to surf today, you need to consider where you are going to fit in.

It's sometimes difficult to accept that the break you're looking at on the day might not be the right place to go out and surf – you're there and you want to paddle. But by going out somewhere that is too tough for you in an attempt to advance your skills, you will endanger yourself and others. Equally, by trying to surf hard somewhere that is actually mellow and full of beginners, you'll find yourself profoundly irritated by the other water users as well as annoying them with your aggressive attitude. A lot of the etiquette that is accepted practice for all surfers is actually impossible to apply if you are hopelessly out of your depth. It is also true to say that even if you play the game correctly, less experienced surfers may be physically unable to. So this rule goes a long way towards avoiding a conflict between riders of differing attitudes and abilities.

Which means, don't take a wave once another surfer has claimed it by taking off in a better or more critical position.

'Dropping in' and 'snaking' are two extremely common ways in which we ruin each other's rides in the surf. They are different types of interference by one surfer on another, and are both usually motivated by greed.

The drop-in happens like this: Surfer A is closest to the peak of the wave, so he paddles for and catches it in the critical position, only to find that Surfer B - the dropper-in - is also paddling for the wave, from further out on the shoulder. Surfer A is then blocked from continuing a successful ride. They may then collide with each other, accidentally or deliberately, and it's unlikely that either will be able to ride the wave. At some critical surf spots, either or both surfers may even be physically endangered as a result.

Drop-ins can and often do happen accidentally. Sometimes you're so focussed on your take-off that you just don't see the other rider. They can also happen through misunderstandings. But they also happen because people just really want to take the wave, and want to believe that it's OK to do so - it isn't.

To avoid dropping in, use the three L's; Look, Listen, and Learn.

■ Look inside, both inshore of you and along the wave to the pocket, and make sure that no one in a better position than you is going for the wave.

■ Listen for a warning – a whistle, or call of "mine!" or something similar.

■ Learn from your mistakes - if you do drop in on somebody, make sure you get off the wave straight away. Go over and say that you're sorry, and make sure the other rider's OK with it before you go to catch more waves.

You might see surfers deliberately taking off and riding together quite happily sometimes. Don't think that means it's OK to drop in – they are probably friends doing it for fun. Or they might just be making the best of a ride already ruined by an accidental drop-in. Doesn't mean they want to ride with you, far from it!

A less obvious, but more deliberate interference is to snake another surfer. This move is very bad form, a nasty exploitation of the widely accepted drop-in rule, and is usually practised by skilful and competitive surfers. Snaking happens like this: Surfer A, who has correctly waited for his turn in the line-up, begins to paddle for the wave. Surfer B (the aggressor) waits until A's totally focussed on his take-off, then paddles quickly around him and takes off inside, claiming the wave. If both surfers end up riding, it looks as though A has dropped in and is in the wrong, but both people, and usually most observers, know that it isn't so.

The big difference between snaking and dropping in, is that snaking is almost never →

accidental. This makes it even more annoying, and it is tempting to confront the offending surfer. But it's better not to react if you can help it – snaking is deliberate and greedy but it probably isn't personal. By having an argument you may make it so, and that isn't usually the way forward. If you find yourself being regularly snaked by a lot of surfers, you may be taking off too far from the peak for them to realise that you are going to surf in the critical part, a common habit for kayakers. Taking off deeper and better will claim the wave – if you can't it might be time to look at the first rule again!

03 give way when paddling out

This is about having the respect not to spoil other people's rides, and it is also about safety. Once someone is up and surfing they should be allowed to enjoy the wave to the full – don't get in their way.

It doesn't make any sense to try to paddle out through the impact zone anyway. That's got to be the hardest and most dangerous way to get back to the line-up. Anyway, not all surfers in the water will have the skills or the inclination to avoid you as you bob in their path like a tethered buoy. If there is a rip or better still a dry paddle-out (sometimes called a transit) then use it – nobody is going to be riding there. Make sure you can see where people are riding, and stay as far away as you can when you paddle out. Most importantly, recognize that the right of way always belongs to the surfer riding in.

Sometimes this doesn't seem possible. For instance, on a beach-break, where the waves break right across and the rideable sections are all over the place. Tough luck – suck it up. If you can't paddle out without potentially interfering with other people's rides, you can't paddle out. It's not their problem. It is yours. Go somewhere else.

■ If you find yourself caught inside the white water, don't cut across another rider's charc in an attempt to get to the green part of the wave; maintain a safe position out of everyone's way, punching or jumping the white water until the set passes, and then go again, heading out of the impact zone if possible. Paddling into the path of a surfer in the critical part of the wave in order to save yourself from a kicking is totally unacceptable.

■ Never block a surfer's attempted take-off by paddling in front of or under him. It doesn't matter whether you think he can catch the wave or not. It's incredibly rude as it will at best interfere with his ride, and obviously very dangerous if he lands on top of you.

Many kayakers completely fail to notice the fact that most of the surfers in the line-up are taking turns. It's not just about who is in the best position to take the wave, it's also about whose turn it is.

Exactly how this is done is not so obvious. You don't take a ticket and wait for your number to be called out. But you should be able to grasp what is going on if you take your time and watch and learn.

At a reef-break with a consistent pattern and take-off zone, the normal situation is for everyone to take their turn. This is complicated by the fact that a surfer might choose not to take his turn on a particular wave, allowing someone else to go instead. Whether he goes to the back of the queue or not will depend on the group dynamics, and this can only be understood by watching the body language and behaviour of the line-up. It's usually fairly clear, and as long as it isn't too crowded everyone can see who's up to go next in the group of surfers who find themselves in a viable position for each wave.

At a point-break it might work a little differently. There could be a number of rideable sections. Inevitably there will be groups of surfers trying to ride each one of them, as if they were separate breaks, and that works fine, as long as they look up the line to make sure no one is going to ride into their section from the previous one. The most common mistake here is pre-emptive paddling; Surfer A is coming down the line from a long way back, and Surfer B – guessing that A won't make the section - begins to paddle for the wave. As A approaches, B drops back; but he's probably already bumped A's charc unless A is very skilful, and/or psychologically extremely strong. Usually A then wipes out or is caught inside, and the rest of the wave goes to waste.

■ Beach-breaks tend to be a bit more transient. There will be lots of different peaks and hence take-off zones. But in each of these zones, the transient nature of the waves might mean that although it's your turn for priority, the next set puts someone else in a better position. Don't be tempted to snake them because it was your turn – take the rough with the smooth.

Beach-breaks can also call for peak etiquette. If you are in position for a really good two-way peak (called an A-frame) with another surfer alongside you, you should choose to go in opposite directions. The trick here is to speak out, and quickly clarify what you are both planning to do. If you both want to go one way, the priority reverts to the normal drop-in rule.

■ Backdoor entry: Sometimes it's possible to get to the take-off spot by launching off rocks or paddling around from another beach. You shouldn't use this way of getting to the line-up as a way of jumping the queue. It's just like taking a river wave from upstream when there are people waiting in the eddy – super-bad form, unless you are invited to do it. Also, having not paddled into the line-up and →

sensed the vibe (see 5) you will at best be seen as an intruder to the scene, and probably cause instant bad feeling.

All of this etiquette tends to go awry if the break is too crowded or if a lot of waves are going unridden because people are failing to catch them or trying to take off too deep. Frustration will begin to build up and people won't see why they should wait their turn or give way to another surfer. If the etiquette of wave sharing just isn't happening, there is very little you can do about it. Just stick to the rules yourself, and hope you can be a good influence. If the situation doesn't get better, maybe then it's time to move on. At least that way you can help with the overcrowding problem!

05 | respect the vibe

You have to get a feel for the attitude in the line-up, and accept it.

From one hour to the next, and from day to day, the attitude or 'vibe' of the line-up can be different. Clearly, the wave conditions can be a contributory factor, but the population of the line-up more so. If you sit out the back for a long time you will notice how the vibe changes as different groups of people come and go at various times of day and states of tide. Surfers of varying age groups, abilities and backgrounds will bring their own attitude to the line-up and subtly alter the mix.

Since you have no real idea what the vibe is going to be it's important to take the time to observe and respond accordingly. The folks already in the line-up will have formed their own bond and system of wave sharing. In this situation, there's nothing worse than one newbie blundering in and upsetting the accepted order.

Before taking any waves, you should always attempt to gain a feel for the vibe in the line-up. Here are some of the ways you might do this:

■ Paddle up to the pack and (with some eye-contact and a smile) say "Hi!" You will instantly get a feel for the vibe just from the instinctive reaction of the other people out there. If they respond amicably and make subtle adjustments to their posture or position in the line-up, you're in the game. If they ignore you, or say something unenthusiastic or downright nasty, move away or surf a different peak. They may accept you once you've shown them a decent ride.

■ Watch and listen. Some crowds are full of shouty people who call out to each other all the time. This kind of crowd is aggressive, →

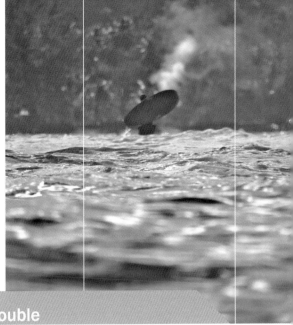

and there are always people competing with each other for a ride. In mellower line-ups, single surfers are given a clear take-off with unspoken good grace. Quiet behaviour is a good sign. Most skilled but mellow surfers are communing with the ocean, not their fellow man. You can get to grips with all of this just by sitting out back for a few minutes, watching, listening and learning.

06 | always help a surfer in trouble

But don't put yourself in difficulties too. Two surfers in trouble are much worse than one.

Surfing is not a dangerous sport per se, but you should always be aware that when we're playing in the water we are not in our natural element. If things do go wrong, it can become a potential drowning incident. Add to that the fact that we often surf in remote places a long way from any help, and that anyone who does come to our aid is also encumbered by having to deal with the waves and water also, and you can see how a small error might become a big problem.

The best way to deal with this situation is if we can all rely on each other in the water. Watch out for other people, and if someone seems to be in trouble, swing into action without delay. Time really is the enemy when someone is tired or injured in the water. Do whatever you can to get help or to get the victim to safety as quickly as possible, before the situation escalates.

It's a good idea to go on a first aid course and acquire a good grasp of resuscitation skills. It can also be very useful to practise trying to rescue people by towing or carrying them with your kayak.

■ If you're a beginner, always try to surf in view of a lifeguard position, or have a buddy on the beach - never surf alone.

The term 'local' doesn't refer to where someone lives, but to the time they have spent committed to a particular surf spot.

If a surfer has surfed a particular spot for a long time, there will be a lot of history and memories associated with it. Every break has its heroes and villains, its triumphs and tragedies. In particular there will be friendships that are inextricably tied to that spot, and traditions that revolve around those relationships. You, as a visiting kayaker, don't know about any of this stuff.

The further you travel from your regular haunts, the bigger the problem becomes. Travel really far afield and cultural differences add to your lack of history there. This can only be overcome by the nurture of trust between a traveller and the locals. And that can sometimes take more time than you have.

It is important, therefore, that the kayak surfer observe the following when travelling to the surf:

■ Take your time. However long or short a time it has taken you to get to the break, it's important to watch and learn for a good long time if you are not a local. Seriously, at least an hour. See where people are riding, how they are riding, and most importantly who is getting the waves.

■ Don't go out in a big group. There are few things worse than six or more kayakers all going out together in the surf. If there are only a few surfers out, consider going out just two at a time. If it is looking really crowded, why add to the problem? You have as much right to a surf as anyone, but believe me when I say it is often better to hold back.

■ Let the locals set the pace. While these ten rules of surfing are widely publicized and generally accepted in most places, the exact way in which they are applied can vary from one locale to another. It's your responsibility to fit in with whatever the locals do. Watch them closely and see if you can work out what is going on. For instance, are the locals deferring to that guy because he's a hot pro and they want to watch him ride? Or because he's threatened them, and they know he's just served time for violent crime? To get a handle on this you may have to sit out there without catching any waves. After a while the locals may actually invite you to take a turn!

■ Do not try to out-surf the locals. It will only cause bad feeling if you do. If you think you are better than they are, try to learn from them what they do have to offer, a superior understanding of local conditions and other useful stuff like which is the best bar in town and where is it safest to park your car.

■ Leave the place clean. Not just in terms of never leaving rubbish behind – that common courtesy should be a given. But try to leave on a good note. Anything bad you do will add to any existing bad feeling towards kayakers. →

Anything good, clearly, will make kayakers more quickly and easily accepted at that spot in the future. So be nice, apologize to anyone you dropped in on, thank everyone for the waves they gave you, and make good anything that could be seen as a negative aspect of your visit.

08 | don't take advantage

In particular of the fact that in your kayak you can catch waves more easily than someone on a board, but also of your status, fitness, strength and skill.

A kayaker is at a significant advantage over almost every other type of surfer. Not only can you paddle out more quickly, but you can catch waves more easily too. Perhaps even more important, you can charge around the break like a mad thing, getting into the best possible position for sets and getting way more rides than anyone else without appearing to drop in or snake.

It is human nature to use your advantages, but that doesn't mean that it's a good idea. It won't go unnoticed, and it will cause a huge amount of bad feeling towards you in particular and kayakers in general.

Surfing etiquette therefore dictates that you become aware of your advantages and the responsibilities that are associated with them.

■ The Alpha-Local should understand that although visiting surfers in particular have a responsibility to respect the locals, they also have a right to come and surf in 'his' spot if they want to. He should look out for those surfers who don't know the hazards of the spot as well as he does, and passing on a few pearls of wisdom about the best waves and other hot tips wouldn't go amiss either. He should be a good example to everyone in the line-up and should uphold the local etiquette and wave-sharing rhythm. However generous he is to other surfers he is still pretty much guaranteed to get the best choice of waves when he wants it!

■ The Long-board or Kayak Surfer understands that his extra speed gives him an unfair advantage when it comes to catching waves and should make sure that he doesn't use it to get more than his fair share. He should also make sure he doesn't jump the queue or whatever system exists in the line-up by virtue of being able to paddle out or around the break more quickly than other surfers.

■ The Pro Kayaker (or surfer for that matter) should be aware that his skill level gives him many of the same advantages that superior equipment (like a faster boat) would and in the same way should not use these advantages to get more waves. He should also realise that, like the Alpha-Local he is looked up to by many others in the line-up and has a responsibility to show a good example. He will also be expected to pass on some of his superior skill and knowledge to surfers less able than himself. He must also be aware that while →

everyone likes to watch an extremely skilled rider perform, it can be a bit rude to show off and it may actually intimidate other riders into submission or to handing the Pro waves when it is not really his turn.

■ The Bigger, Older, Stronger or More Confident Person should realise that these attributes can be a bit scary and intimidating, especially to young kids although they might choose not to show it. This intimidation, although not deliberate, can result in other surfers letting him take more waves in the same way as the Pro. It's important not to allow this to happen, and that such a person uses his attributes as a force for good, in looking after the inexperienced or less strong and confident riders.

09 take responsibility for your equipment

If it is not properly maintained and controlled a kayak (or a surfboard) can be a very dangerous instrument, and can cause serious physical harm to people and equipment.

■ First and simplest to recall: never let your kayak go. You should consider the possibility that if you can't negotiate a surf spot without throwing your boat away, the spot may not be for you. Make sure you personally are up to the job, and also that your paddle, spraydeck (skirt) and other equipment is not going to let you down and force you to wet exit.

■ Second, be sure you can get off the broken waves if you are caught inside. Everyone has a physical limit – the better and stronger you are, the larger the waves you can surf with absolute confidence so that if it all comes crashing down, you will be able to get off without careering dangerously into other people.

■ Beginners: It's tough I know, and seems unfair. But it's just totally unacceptable to bail out of your boat and then fail to hold onto it, or to stay in the boat and bounce around in the white water, unless you are in a super-controlled situation with no innocent water users inshore of you. If you can't ensure other people's safety this way, find somewhere safer to learn how!

In addition to this you must ensure that you maintain your boat and paddle with a view to ensuring others' safety as well as your own. Fins or paddle-blade edges, sharp bits of damaged boat, and pointy or hard unprotected tips can be dangerous to other surfers too.

If you have a collision that damages someone else's boat or board, make sure you offer to pay for or repair the damage. It's a good idea to have third party liability insurance in case of any unfortunate accident. →

By the same virtue, we can expect all surfers to be as considerate as we will be. Board-riders, in particular, should not kick off in a manner that launches their board out to the limit of their leash, thus potentially endangering anyone within a diameter of ten metres! If surfers aren't skilled enough to control their board on exit, they should go and learn how, somewhere less crowded...

10 | chill out and enjoy everybody's rides

You're there to ride some waves, but so is everyone else. Enjoy what they do too and we'll all have more fun.

■ Interact positively with other surfers and you will get more and better rides, and have a wider range of experience. Go to different spots, surf at different times of day. Understand how other people ride and why they ride that way.

■ Give other people rides and the benefit of the doubt, perhaps a few more than their fair share. It places you on the moral high ground when you really want to take a slightly controversial wave yourself, and it's a deposit in the karma-bank for the time when you make a mistake. Other surfers will think "Well, he dropped in that time, but he's been super-nice all day so I don't mind".

■ Smile. It makes so much difference. It will make you feel more positive, and you will enjoy other people's rides as much as your own. More to the point, you will enjoy your bad rides as much as your good ones as long as you remember to smile. It will make you much less intimidating to other surfers, and you'll come across as more approachable which enables you to interact with other surfers as described above. It will defuse the potential for confrontation when you have to ask someone not to drop in on you again, too!

If you can stick to these ten rules you should not experience any of the problems that kayakers traditionally complain of when trying to surf in the 'mixed company' of shortboarders, longboarders, bodyboarders and the like. Any negativity that kayakers might have experienced or continue to experience is a direct result of failing to conform to basic surfing etiquette and expectation, not from being in a kayak. Remember, it's not what you ride, it's how you ride!

■ WAVES, like life, have an inescapable cycle of ebb and flow, yin and yang. Everything comes and goes in waves. Do not cling to the wave after its time is done, and that will not bother you. Welcome the waves when the set comes, and let them go gracefully when it is over. There is nothing you can do to stop it, so the only choice you have is how graciously and skilfully you deal with it.

Like many things, waves often come in sets of three. If being caught inside would be a bad thing, don't take the first one of the set. For a variety of reasons the third one is usually the biggest, but it often pays to try for the second wave. Miss the third and you miss out completely.

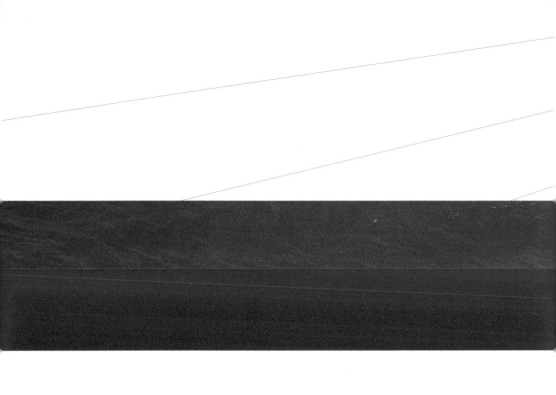

CORE MOVES

COREMOVES

Top to bottom riding using top turns, bottom turns and cutbacks is what dynamic surfing is all about. The skills required are quite basic ones for a kayaker who has the competence to take a boat out in the surf. But they are key, and you must learn to apply them in a wide range of surf conditions and circumstances. These skills will form the core of your repertoire and will be in-core-porated (sic) into every ride. Without them you cannot ride, and cannot begin to consider being in a position to be radical.

The bottom turn is the classic, archetypal surfing manoeuvre. It's been said that you can tell everything about someone's surfing just by watching how they make a bottom turn. Bit of a generalisation, I'd say, but if you can't make a dramatic opening statement to set the scene, what can you do?

A bottom turn, clearly, is a turn you make at the bottom of the wave. But that actually doesn't describe it very well. Could be anything, that... It is the turn you make to convert your motion down the wave into motion up the wave.

bottom turn

When you get to the **bottom of** the wave you have **a lot of sp**eed, but you ride **onto a part** of the wave that is **not very ste**ep, so if you dither **you will los**e it all. You need to **try to carry** as much speed as **you can ba**ck up to the steep **part of the** face, so that you **can accele**rate again using **the magic** G+S (Gravity plus **Steepness**). So, a bottom turn **must alwa**ys be smooth. You **might snap** or force a top turn or a cutback, but a bottom turn must flow. How tightly you turn and how much you lean over will, I'm afraid, have to be learnt by experiment in your particular boat, but the rule of two thumbs is:

A TURN SLOWLY AND SMOOTHLY FOLLOWING THE NATURAL TURNING RADIUS OF YOUR RAIL.

B LEAN OVER AS FAR AS YOU CAN WITHOUT THE BRAKES COMING ON.

I would also recommend minimising the braking effect of the paddle. You will probably need it for support, but try to keep it planing on the surface rather than submerged. And here's a hot tip – if your blade is trailing near the tail, the weight you put on it can reduce the pressure on the stern of the boat, and that might mean less trailing edge downforce, and more speed. Cool! Mess about with this and see if you can get it to work.

I always have my weight as far forward as I can during a bottom turn, trying to engage the more curved part of the rail at the front of the hull. I also tend to keep the hull fairly flat through the turn, but hang my body weight out towards the wave, because this keeps the pressure on the up-wave rail, but keeps the sides of the boat out of the water. If you drop your knee into the water the brakes come on rather suddenly! A fairly flat ride also keeps all your fins in the water, and it is during the bottom turn that you most feel the need for fins. So that would seem to be a good idea.

Remember to ease out of your bottom turn before you end up carving over the back of the wave. A smooth exit from the turn is as important as the turn itself and you'll probably need to start it as you leave the bottom of the turning arc, as your chi sits patiently at the lip, endowing your charc with infinite intent as the possibilities for a top turn unfold.

top turn

Top turns are important too. Quite a lot of surfers don't really make a top turn – rather they just float along between bottom turns, slowly succumbing to gravity. The top turn is critical to high energy riding, but it can take many forms. What is always present is the need for excellent anticipation and timing.

You cannot emulate your bottom turn in a top turn. If you simply weight-shift onto your down-wave rail and use your paddle for support, you will make a good turn, as long as you have a lot of speed and the wave is dribbly and non-critical. But in most circumstances, on a steep face anyway, you would be upside down if you tried to do this. Think about it. So normally I would pre-rotate for the turn as I ride up the face, keeping the boat on its climbing rail (the up-wave one). Only once your chi, charc and intent are committed to making a turn can you relinquish your grip by releasing the edge and flattening the hull to the wave.

The turn could be: (a) long, smooth and driving, carrying a lot of speed into the next turn, or (b) a quick snap, killing some speed but establishing a position very high in the wave. You've traded kinetic energy for potential, in the latter case. It's really a stall, almost a cutback. In (a) you are actually reliant on your speed, because it will be the centrifugal force of the turn that stops you falling over, rather than the paddle blade. In (b) you will lose that support as you stall, but the snappy turn means that your body will be over the boat again before you have time to realise there is nothing holding you up. And falling is all about realising there is nothing supporting you... I'm convinced.

If you do a long, flowing turn, you should pay attention to the natural radius of your boat's carving rail, which will vary according to angle of attack, i.e. how much edge you apply. If you try to turn more quickly than this radius, you will lose speed, and maybe you would have been better off snapping it around, accepting the loss of speed.

A snap will require a bit of effort with the down-wave paddle blade. In fact, on a steep wave I sometimes launch my entire weight onto the blade. Normally when you are sweeping the paddle forwards to achieve a turning moment, it is a lot more effective to start near the tail and sweep away from the

boat. But remember, we're not on the flat here. You could easily be wedging the tail into the wave, or prying the nose down into the water. Place the paddle in the water in a non-draggy manner, get some feedback, and then do what you must to make the turn.

With enough momentum you can make a top turn without using your paddle, and it's an interesting thing to practise anyway. You need to be able to lean into the turn enough that the centrifugal force is supporting you, just as you do when going around a bend on your bike. If you mess it up and lose all your speed you'll fall in, but how do you know you're having fun if you don't get wet?

radical top turn
& off-the-lip

Although the top turn is a basic part of your surfing repertoire, it is probably the move most often associated with super-radical behaviour. After all, you can afford to go a bit crazy. Whether the move is functional as well as funky or not, you are still going to be at the top of the wave when it's over, and that gives you maximum potential energy even if your killer turn attempt has thrown away all your speed.

What kind of radicalism am I talking about here? An aerial (I'm talking a proper fly-in-the-sky aerial here, not some butt-bounce, flip or freefall that happens to get your boat out of the water) is a top turn. Just a kind of super-elevated, alpha-top turn. See pp122-123 for more details. Or a more regular example (and actually the same move from a riding perspective) is the off-the-lip, which takes a top turn as far as it can be taken without breaking free into the realm of air.

If you do an extremely aggressive off-the-lip top turn and commit heavily to your down-wave blade, you may find your fins or chines

release and the boat turns very suddenly, the tail slashing through the air behind the wave. This is a Slash. It tends to happen most if your weight has stayed forward as you ride into the lip. This can be a very satisfying and spectacular thing, but may also kill all your speed, and/or result in you falling off the back (or the front) of the wave depending how steep and throwing the wave is. If it works out, concentrate on riding away from the inevitable bow-burying moment which can become terminal if your body language is out of sync with your charc.

It is interesting to practise top turns where you keep your weight on the up-wave rail throughout. The only thing you need to do differently is switch to a down-wave blade sooner, perhaps even flirting with the dreaded stern-rudder, and perhaps let your weight come back earlier in the move. You may find this technique useful in extremely steep or barrelling surf conditions. Experiment also with slides and reverts which can be used as top turns too.

■ ON YOUR FIRST ATTEMPT TURN EARLY ON THE WAVE AND DON'T WORRY ABOUT HITTING THE LIP. AS YOU GAIN CONFIDENCE, TRY TO HIT THE LIP CLOSER AND CLOSER TO WHERE THE WAVE IS PITCHING.

■ TRY ONLY SMALL WAVES UNTIL YOU ARE CONFIDENT WITH YOUR SKILLS.

■ FOCUS ON YOUR RAIL.

how to do an off-the-lip

A Drop in a wave, and execute a solid bottom turn (see bottom turn p52). As you finish the turn, the pressure will be on your up-wave rail.

B Redirect the pressure to the opposite rail, i.e. your down-wave rail.

C Keep your body fairly upright, even leaning into the wave. Just use your knees to drop the rail, and keep your blade in the wave to resist any tendency for the bow to drop.

D As you go up the wave, pre-rotate so your chest is facing down, and switch your blade to the down-wave side. As you approach the lip, let your weight come slowly back. Keep pressure on the downward rail, and turn hard as you hit the lip of the wave.

E Drop back down the face of the wave, keeping your weight back so you are ready to throw yourself forward if it looks like the nose will bury.

F Prepare to do another bottom turn. Remember you'll be carrying a lot more kinetic energy into this one!

G Repeat until the wave is no longer rideable or until you achieve Nirvana or an overwhelming urge to hit the bar.

BELOW - Maintaining ride speed, Bill turns a cutback 01 & 02 into a roundhouse 01 - 04 (see over)

01

CORE MOVES   cutback

cutback

The cutback is a many-splendoured thing. When surfers see a kayaker take a wave, they wonder whether he'll find the power-pocket and turn to ride with it. When he does, cool – he knows how to surf. But it's when he makes his first successful cutback that they think "He really can surf!"

The purpose of the cutback is simply to return you to the highest energy part of the wave (the power-pocket) when the wave has slowed, or 'backed off' as it is sometimes called. The trick is to get back there without throwing away any ride energy. If the wave is backing off, the last thing you want to do is waste the energy already gained from the wave. So, rather than slowing down, you should keep your speed, just reduce your velocity along the wave by making a turn back towards the break.

The basic cutback simply takes the form of a top turn that is held until the boat is riding straight to shore. You wait for the foam-pile to catch up with you, and then allow the boat to turn away from it again to ride along in the power-pocket. Assuming that we are talking about a fairly soft wave. If the wave is big, steep or pitching, you don't want to point straight down-wave for fear of purling or bouncing out of control down the front and losing your potential energy with which to regain the ride.

If however, the wave is not too steep, you can make the turn, hang quite high in the wave as you look at the oncoming whitewash, and then drop again to go kinetic as you make the transition back into normal ride mode. Sometimes the cutback will be really subtle, perhaps just a top turn held for a fraction of a second longer, or with the boat a little flatter - a carefully managed stall high in the wave more than anything else. The expert will sometimes make very small adjustments to maintain position in the most critical part of the wave, especially if the conditions are either very soft and mushy and won't support big turns, or when the wave is so critical that major direction changes might lead to disaster!

On the other hand, you will often see aggressive hi-energy riders making huge, gouging cutbacks as they whack from base to lip and back again – if you can keep the speed and power of your ride maxed out in this way, all the better. The gentle approach is very subtle, but it is ultimately going to lead only to moderate-looking rides. Mind you, a moderate or even downright wibbly-looking ride on a hot, super-critical break can be tenfold more worthy than banging off the lip of two foot mush!

Roundhouse Tips:

■ DON'T TRY TO START A ROUNDHOUSE CUTBACK FROM THE BOTTOM OF THE WAVE. ALTHOUGH YOU ARE OFTEN AT THE BOTTOM WHEN YOU REALISE YOU HAVE EXCESS SPEED. RIDE TO THE TOP BEFORE YOU LOOK BACK AT THE POCKET AND INITIATE THE MANOEUVRE.

■ IF THE WAVE IS VERY STEEP OR PITCHING, YOU WON'T PULL OFF A ROUNDHOUSE CUTBACK. IF YOU DON'T LAND ON YOUR HEAD AFTER THE FIRST TURN, THE SECOND WILL SURELY BE YOUR UNDOING.

radical cutback

PICTURED ABOVE - BILL POWERS UP THE RAIL AND PREPARES TO SWITCH EDGES IN MID ROUNDHOUSE CUTBACK.

SLASH - If you want to make a roundhouse style move, but are a bit too close to the break or just want a variety injection, you could try slashing the tail for the first turn (see p112). This will kill a lot of speed, but it's a cutback, so why not live a little? If you lose all your speed you may need to rebound from the pile rather than carving the rest of the cutback (see p66 Rebounds). This Slash/ Bounce combo can look quite cool actually, as long as you don't do it all the time!

WRAPAROUND - Carve back to the pocket like a roundhouse, but instead of turning back away from the white stuff you carry on carving up and around until you're riding facing the way you started in a kind of off-the-lip. This is also called a carved 360°.

ROUNDHOUSE - This extremely useful cutback can be confusing because different groups of people define it in various ways. Some describe something like a carved 360°. Others use it to mean any cutback where you make two distinct turns or edge changes. And white water kayakers often use it to describe a low-angle blunt, which has very few cutback-like properties at all (see off-side spins p115). I've gone for the meaning that I hear more often than the others – a cutback where you turn to establish a new ride direction towards the break, and then turn away again to ride the normal way. Two full 180° turns.

A Ride to the top of the wave and look over your down-wave shoulder at the pocket.

B If you're still sure you want to roundhouse - make a top turn and hold it. Don't rail over super-aggressively, but stay on the down-wave edge until you are riding towards the break and it has become your up-wave edge.

C Make another top turn immediately. This time rail over as much as you dare because the whitewash will probably hit you and if it hits you when you are flat, your fins/chines/rails will cavitate and you won't turn.

D Hold your second top turn until you are riding away from the power pocket again, but level the boat as soon as possible because you really need to accelerate here – you've just cut back deep into the critical section!

A You're in the open face of the wave with a lot of speed. So bury your down-wave rail in the water and hold it through the cutback. Keep your down-wave blade in top-turn mode but don't let it brake you.

C Turn your head and lock your eyes on the whitewash.

D Turn up the wave with your weight coming back and try to unweight your boat so you 'hop up', allowing your nose to ride on top of the pile.

E Push the tail around once you hit the foam, by sweeping the same blade forward and slightly releasing the edge.

F Continue the turn back down the face as you rebound from the break. Timing is critical, and where you look is where you'll be in a second's time... The real trick with this move is not to lose speed in the first turn. You need to ride a long way down the wave to give yourself room. Or you need a very big wave and absolutely no fear... or sense.

slides

Most surfing manoeuvres are carved, and this tends to maintain direction, energy and control. But sometimes it pays to play fast and loose, and let things slip a little.

So let's imagine... you're riding along in the time-honoured manner, you've ended up at the top of the wave for one reason or another, and you'd prefer to be at the bottom, but you don't want to generate more speed than you have already. You just release the carving rail, flatten off a little

and slip sideways down the wave. Rolling your weight back onto the up-wave rail to stop the slide.

If you have a lot of fin, this may work a little differently. My boat just won't slide at all unless you deliberately cavitate the fins by bumping them sideways with a bit of body language. Once they've released, though, the boat slides down-wave like any other. If the fins don't fully release, the nose may drop without the tail doing so.

Especially if the fins are really far back (mine are). But this can be good too. Sometimes the shape of the wave just lends itself to this kind of half turn, half slide.

You can do another type of slide out of a bottom turn. Flatten the boat off early and do the bump-your-hips-sideways thing, and the tail will break away, leaving you pointing more up-wave than you would have been. This has the advantage that it is easier to ride away from than

CORE MOVES slides

carving a super-tight turn up the wave, which, because we can't unweight the ends of the boat the way a board-rider can, often leaves us in an untenable position.

It can be hard to regain rail control after a slide. Slowly increasing the amount of rail applied, as described in the first example, is a safe way to do it, but often lacks energy or just takes a couple of seconds longer than you feel it should. Deliberately rolling onto the rail you're sliding towards, however, is a super-radical technique that can snap you straight back into carving in a most excellent way. Or trip you up instantly and extremely hard, if you aren't too good at it! Leaning your body towards your leading edge first, then bringing the leading rail into play after can be a good way to make it work. But practice is the the only sure way to get a reliable result.

Slides, like spins, can look a bit pathetic if they're not executed with conviction. But commit to them as you would to more aggressive moves, and they can be very cool, especially if used as a deliberate break from the norm between more hard charging manoeuvres. It makes the ride better visually if you can keep 'em functional though, since like most surfing techniques they don't tend to be aesthetically pleasing if they are done pointlessly or for no apparent reason.

If you use a trick because you had plenty of spare time in the ride, it doesn't look clever – it just draws attention to the fact that your ride was so slack and uncritical, it had plenty of spare time in it!

rebounds

or bouncers, as they are sometimes called...

At some point you are bound to find it useful to bounce off the foam pile. This can be done after a cutback (turn back towards the break and then bounce off it to ride away in the power-pocket) or sometimes it can be nice to ride ahead of the pocket into an oncoming or closing section. Bouncing off the whitewash as you try to carve around a foam-ball is another useful application of the rebound.

Whatever your reason, it's a fairly easy thing to do, but hard to do with style. The key in most boats is to rebound off the hull, not the side of the boat. This way, it looks like the breaking wave simply turbocharged your carve. Otherwise, it can appear as though you blundered into an unstoppable force of nature, and rather luckily managed to wobble away from the impact in vaguely the right direction. Which is considerably less cool.

As with so many moves, timing is key. Foam is highly aerated water, so it hits you softer and later than you'd probably expect. Don't write to me about this when you get hospitalised by a macking lip, there are limits to everything you

know. Even something soft can hurt you if it's going really fast. Anyway, the first few times you will find you rebound later and deeper in the pile than expected. A good trick is to go in fairly flat, then increase your rail quickly to let the foam hit your hull. This way, you are calling the shots about when the pile slams you away, and the timing will feel more natural. Maybe.

If you are fighting your way along a breaking section to regain the shoulder, having failed to carve your way around in one go, you may want to carve into the pile on your down-wave edge to get as high in the foam as you can without falling foam grabbing a rail. Switching edges as the climb energy plays out may work well – so too may staying on the same rail throughout, but it's not that stable. Whatever edge you use, remember to anticipate the boat's reaction with your body. Look where you're going next and pre-rotate your body to follow your gaze. You need to stay well ahead with this in any move where the wave adds energy to your charc, because it may happen later than you expect, but it will happen quickly when it does!

PICTURED BELOW - Despite being massive and brutal, this wave is a classic 'ride ahead and off the end' scenario.

CORE MOVES   exiting

When the wave is done, you'll want to make a deliberate move to get off. Sometimes being able to do this is essential to your continued well-being. More often it is just better not to bimble into the soup, or continue past the point where paddling out again is a reasonable undertaking. Either way some sort of strategy would be in order.

exiting

No, I don't mean getting out of your boat. I mean getting your boat out of the wave.

BACK OFFS

Some waves typically back off into the beach-break, which means that the wave simply dies under you. Bargain.

RIDE OFF THE END

We'd all love to ride breaks where you can just surf off the shoulder straight into a deep channel every time. Unfortunately, very few of us get to. And many of the breaks where this is possible are hot, critical, do-not-screw-up type of situations, which tends to have a de-mellowifying effect on the proceedings.

JUMP OFF THE END

There are many top reef-breaks which bowl, rather than breaking in a straight line parallel to shore. If they don't facilitate riding the whole bowl and off the end, you will need to charge ahead of the break far enough to be able to ride up and over the wave before the lip pitches too far. This is rarely easy and never safe in this, the gnarliest type of break around.

PUNCH OUT

You realise that you aren't going over the top but you need out. Make as if to carve off but carry on railing over harder and harder right into the lip or falling water 01 - 02. Punch your paddle end-on through the back of the wave and stick your head through in the same direction 03. Keep the paddle low along the boat - if it gets slapped by the lip you don't want to get hit in the face. Do not let the boat level out or all the water falling on you will take you down.

CARVE OFF

On waves that end as a close-out, you have to anticipate the end and be ready to carve off before the close. Just as though you were trying for an aerial, charge hard into a bottom turn, hold the rail most of the way up the face, but reach over the lip with your paddle and launch right off the back 01. Best case scenario, you launch into the air and throw a kickflip for good measure 02. Worst case the lip smacks your bow back down again, you go over the falls and get a gnarling.

BAIL OUT

If there is clearly no way to get the boat off the wave, and staying on the wave is undeniably going to result in your getting mashed into a horrible reef or something, consider jumping out of your kayak without further ado. If you are strapped in this isn't really going to happen, but you really should have thought of that first, shouldn't you?

COREINFO

the crystal ball

Many of us have set off for the coast on a Friday night, expecting to spend the weekend ripping it up on a break that puts Pipeline to shame, only to put in more miles than the guys from Endless Summer and still not find a wave worth untying the boats for. But with a little knowledge of weather forecasting, wasted journeys to the coast could be a thing of the past.

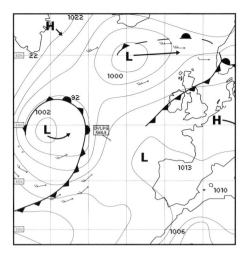

We've all seen numerous articles on surf forecasting and most of us haven't read them, because it seems as though you need an MSc in Meteorology and to have been glued to the weather charts for a fortnight to make head or tail of them. This is a shame, because it's not really that hard to work out what the surf will be doing in a few days time. There are basically three things you need to know.

Let's keep it simple; waves are made by the wind, right? But not by the wind that's blowing at the beach, or even anywhere near the land. The waves are made by strong winds in the middle of the ocean. All you need to do is look at a weather chart with isobars (black lines forming concentric circles like contour lines); in the UK, the BBC TV national weather is ideal. Look at the low-pressure areas. The wind is blowing in an anticlockwise direction around the low, roughly along the isobars, and the closer together the isobars, the stronger the wind. If there is an area where a strong wind is blowing towards your chosen bit of

coast, there will be waves coming your way. It doesn't matter if the waves are being made a thousand miles away, as long as the wind blows them in your direction. Now, the longer the distance over which the wind blows in the right direction, the bigger the waves get. This can happen either because the low is shaped so that the isobars are straight for a long way, or because the low moves along at a similar speed to the waves so that the wind continues to act on them in the same direction.

There are all sorts of fiendishly difficult equations to work out wave height, but you don't need them. Just bear in mind that if there is a low with reasonably tight isobars indicating a useful swell direction, there will be some waves arriving soon. Try to guess how far away it is. Wave energy travels at around 70mph. Now you can work out when the swell will arrive. If the low has very tight isobars, or exists for several days, they will be big waves. If it has either of the above and moves steadily towards the land, they will be very big waves. →

Lows that are deepening over several days give big, solid swells, whereas ones that are filling from adjacent highs tend not to produce anything of note. If you check the weather map regularly, and bear these things in mind, you will quickly build up a feel for the likely wave size at your favourite beaches.

The above enables you to predict a swell, but ideally you want to know the wave quality as well. The perfect wave occurs when the wind direction at the coast is a light offshore. If the wind is onshore, the waves will be messy, and a strong offshore wind makes it hard to take off and can kill the swell if it holds for too long. Look at the weather map again. This time look at the isobars actually crossing your bit of coastline. Remember that the wind blows anticlockwise round a low-pressure area? Well, surprise, it blows clockwise round a high (in the Southern hemisphere it's the other way around)! What we need for good surf is a light local wind, so the isobars here shouldn't be close together. If the local wind derives from a high, that's all the better, because that probably means good weather too.

Bear in mind that if your swell producing area sends waves through an area where the wind is blowing the other way this diminishes the wave size accordingly. That's why we want a strong wind generating swell for several hundred miles, then a light local breeze in the other direction for only a short distance. Secondly, when you look at the usual type of weather map shown on TV or in one of the national newspapers, the world is distorted by the projection they use. A low up by Greenland looks the same distance away from the UK as one due west of us near the edge of the chart, but waves take much longer to arrive from the Greenland low because it is actually quite a bit further away.

I usually watch a national weather forecast on a Wednesday if I'm hoping to surf at the weekend. That's partly because this tends to be the right time scale for Atlantic swells, but also because on a Wednesday where I live they show the expected maps right up to the weekend, so you can see if the weather systems are doing the right things.

Now that you can predict the swell conditions you should be much more likely to find the waves you're looking for. It's still worth calling one of the surf check lines or surfing, pardon the pun, the net for an on-line prediction before you leave, to confirm that the swell is doing what you expect, but remember, surf can pick up or die off in a matter of hours. So what it's doing right now this minute doesn't mean much. Prediction is the name of the game.

WEB WAVES - As we've already mentioned the modern day surfer has the power of the web at their fingertips. There is a plethora of both short and long range surf forecast sites and many UK beaches have a direct link and even web cams to help make your journey worthwhile. We've noted a few useful sites to help you score sweet waves but there are many, many just a surf away...

Check out **WWW.GOATBOATER.COM** for links to some of the best surf prediction resources worldwide, compiled especially for kayak surfers. Alternatively, searching the web can usually yield a local forecast, or a WAM map or forecast (Wave Amplitude Model) from which you can make your own predictions.

Bear in mind that this one can give you an optimistic view of the wave size. Whatever swell it shows on the coast where you surf, expect half that at the beach. This is because the size of the deep ocean swells diminishes that much as it crosses our continental shelf. Also bear in mind that this doesn't apply to small islands not on continental shelves, like the Azores, Hawaii and Tahiti to name but a few. These get the full brunt of the open ocean swell.

MAKING IT

I've talked about how you should ride in the power pocket, and try to stay in this critical, high-energy zone, as it races along the wave. But as anyone who's ever tried it will know, it's more easily said than done. Good carving skills will take care of it as long as the wave doesn't throw you a curve ball, but sadly that's exactly what the wave usually does. So, unlike a river wave, the ocean wave takes focus, timing, and anticipation...

It's easy enough to stay in the pocket of a wave that breaks progressively all the way. Even if some sections are a bit faster and steeper than others, it's usually a simple matter to trim the kayak using normal steering strokes and keep it in the zone. But what happens when the wave suddenly breaks ahead of you, or in the opposite case, backs off completely and leaves you riding out onto the shoulder with lots of speed but nowhere to go? To take care of this we have a bag of work-around tricks, and with experience you can pull out an appropriate strategy as you see what kind of a section you're getting yourself into.

If you're one lucky boater and one of these work-arounds comes good, you're going to ride into the next section with a lot of speed. Which is where you will need a cutback (see p60), otherwise you'll ride out onto a less steep and dynamic part of the wave, losing all your speed. As soon as you're through the quick section, you adjust your velocity along the wave, not by braking (don't throw away your hard-won speed) but by making a turn back into the steep stuff and then back into the ride again, keeping yourself firmly located in the critical zone at all times...

race ahead

If the wave rounds off ahead of you, tucking yourself deep in the pocket is the way to go. But sometimes the wave will wall up big, leaving you with a section that will probably close out. What to do?

Anticipation is the key. If, by observation of how the wave breaks, consideration of other people's rides, or bitter experience of your own, you can tell that the section is going to do that before it

happens, then cut back as deep and high as you can just prior to the section and then set what you guess to be your best descent angle for maximum speed and drive into a bottom turn.

If you haven't premeditated this part of the ride, it may still be possible to anticipate the

fast section by observation – if the top of the wave is not sloping down at all for some distance ahead of you it's a pretty safe bet that it's all gonna come crashing down. It is not always easy to see it though. I have surfed in places (including one of my favourite local breaks) where a fast section looks entirely

01

02

progressive and shouldery – only as you ride into it does the whole twenty metre section suddenly close out!

The key thing is to be in a super-steep critical position at the last possible moment before you race into the section. Most people make the mistake of racing ahead early, but they don't carry enough speed into the manoeuvre from the outset.

The other great rule of thumb is go high. You have to be brave. It will look as though you aren't going to make it, but the correct way to respond to this is to aim for the lip rather than to skulk at the bottom of the wave. If your bottom turns don't take you back to the very lip you are not going to keep your speed for long. "Do, or do not – there is no try" (Yoda I believe) – you must either ride aggressively or straighten off and run for your life. The in-between riding style is limp, unexciting, and largely ineffective...

← Predicting a close-out, Bill trades in all his potential energy for a burst of speed, losing height on the face as he does so but making it ahead of the pitching section to a point where he can go high again...

CARVE AROUND:

It's quite a good idea to look behind you as well as ahead. Quite a few times I've watched myself on video, battling to make a near impossible section as the broken section behind me re-formed into an eminently rideable wave breaking the other way!

There is a world of difference between diving under a falling section to make it through and getting a tube ride. I do the former all the time. The latter occurs only exceptionally, even at some of the best breaks in the world. But sooner or later, if you choose under rather than over or around as your preferred modus operandi in this work-around scenario, the opportunity for tube rides will present itself, so it seems to me worth pursuing, if only for that reason. It is the **wor**k-around most prone to failure, and ends as often as not in a colossal wipe-out, but what the hell. We can dream, can't we?

Here's a thing. Once the wave is steep and pitching, it's pretty hard to ride. The steep face is potentially energy-giving, but the water will be rising up the wave very fast, so you may end up riding low on the face to avoid being sucked over the falls. Which is fine, but ride too low and you may find yourself getting smacked by the falling lip or 'curtain'.

tuck under

MAKING IT   tuck under

Riding high in the steep part of the face provides you with a high speed environment with which to make the section, but you'll need a big wave, or you'll be sticking your head through the roof. It is also very hard to keep your paddle out of harm's way – if it even touches the curtain, you're going down! Obviously, however big the wave, you can't go much more than halfway up the face because it won't be vertical - it'll be past vertical and you'll be upside down!

It seems to me that the recipe for sustained success in this under-the-lip situation is to have a realistic grasp of how long you can hold it together and to straighten off, through the falling curtain if necessary, as soon as you anticipate that the ride is becoming unviable. If you do this with conviction you will make as much of the section as possible while still retaining the option to carve around the rest of it to regain the shoulder.

floater

A great move for making sections that are going to break ahead of you. Floaters don't work if the wave is fluffy or mushy, but a gnarly crashing section can be avoided by simply riding over it on the back of the lip. It's a hot looking trick as well as totally functional.

It'll take a lot of failed attempts to get this. It's a very basic surfboard move but it is soooo difficult in a kayak you hardly ever see anyone do it. It is definitely worth trying though. The floater is good practice for all kinds of other off-the-lip antics and really can save your bacon in barely-makeable, critical breaks.

Floaters, I think, are one of the most useful manoeuvres you can do. It's a good one if you're learning to surf because you can try them in very small waves. Unfortunately they are hard to do in a kayak because of the limited amount of pitch you can generate (see Weight Shift p32). It is doubly unfortunate that if you drop down from a floater in big surf, you can have horrific wipe-outs or even serious injuries, because you have nothing to absorb the shock of landing and you end up, by the very nature of the move, in a very vulnerable position at the bottom of a very energetic bit of wave.

MAKING IT   floater

A When you see a section collapsing in front of you - gather as much speed as possible. Angle your ride up the face and project yourself toward the lip.

B Bend forward as you ride up on top of the lip, and let your weight come back as you get there. This is to try to unweight the hull as best you can.

C Ride flat on the back side of the lip for as long as you can, until you feel your speed starting to diminish. Pre-rotate to face the shore as you do so.

Don't try to steer or edge while you're up on the lip, or you'll lose all your speed in the super-aerated water.

D Make a powerful sweep on the seaward side bringing the bow down the face to start re-entry. This will tend to take your weight back.

E Drop down with the lip and throw your weight forward to try to land fins first.

F If the wave is three foot or over, shout "Ouch!" loudly and try to remember the number of your physiotherapist.

MAKING IT   workin' it

workin' it

Once you have the whole bag of tricks described in the preceding section, and a good handle on fighting for control in the pile, soup or whitewash as it is variously called, you need to develop your instinct for assembling this set of skills into a determined effort to 'make it'.

RULE Nº1 Don't take your eyes off the prize. Focus on the power-pocket where you want to be and don't look up, down or around!

RULE Nº2 Don't give up. Fight for it until it's hopeless and then put a similar amount of effort into getting off the wave quickly!

RULE Nº3 Don't make it too easy! Remember that surfing is all about riding in the critical section, and just because you have the speed/skill/power to get ahead of that section doesn't mean that's either stylish or a ride-enhancing thing to do!

Believe - mingled with our chi and charc is a fair bit of faith. As I have said elsewhere, if you don't think you can do it, you can't do it. Conversely, if you are absolutely certain you can do it, you probably don't have all the facts at your disposal. Believe that you can do it, and your chi will be patiently waiting for you just around the corner where success lives...

it's your call

Sometimes your entire bag of work-around tricks won't offer any solution. Or else you may simply fail to make a section. Unlike a surfboard rider you may not flush deep and take your chances with the hold-down. You may be bundled out of control across the reef, washed over the rocks, or hurled headlong through the mêlée of swimmers or people standing hopefully in waist deep water clutching a variety of surf toys and powerless to move out of your way.

We have a responsibility to be aware of this possibility, and to be willing to accept the consequences of our actions. I am not comfortable with the remotest possibility that my kayak might be propelled by many tons of breaking water into the face

of someone's loved one. My own face being slammed into razor sharp coral only inches under water isn't top of my wish list either.

Many unfortunate surfing situations can be avoided by simply straightening off and riding directly onshore, even in extreme cases, as long as you have the judgement and the skill to stick the move. It's not something we often think of practising, but it might turn out to be the most important move we ever make.

MAKING IT think

think...

I had a moment of instant clarity when I saw this photo. OK, first of all I went "Ooooooh, look at this pretty wave!" and then I had the moment of clarity, which was this:

If you look at the wake (the trail in the water) made by the tail of my kayak, and then you look at the trail made by my paddle, you can see that they curve up the wave at radically different angles. It's something I've thought about before when looking at surfing pictures, but this shot illustrates it particularly well. What does it mean?

Well, if you assume that my boat and my paddle are both charging along the wave at the same speed (and you'll just have to trust me that I know they were), then it means that the water is going up the face of the wave a heck of a lot faster where my paddle's located than it is at the tail of the boat. And that's important.

The reason for this is clear. The stern is by the broken part of the wave, where the top has crashed down leaving only the lower and not very steep part still green. My paddle is right under the pitching part that is just starting to throw the lip right over my head. So the water is rushing upwards real fast to fuel that lip. Whereas behind me where it isn't so steep, it's rising more gently.

That's all good. What does it mean? It means you have to feel that stuff through the hull of your boat and your paddle, that's for sure. Because if the water at the nose is going up faster than that at the tail we're going to spin right off the back, aren't we? And it isn't always going to be that way around – it's pretty likely you might ride with the stern in a steeper part of the wave than the bow sometimes. One reason I ride with the paddle up in the wave as much as possible, is to feel the speed differential between the blade and what I'm feeling through the boat. If you ride on a down-wave stern rudder it's not telling you anything new, now, is it?

And the more radical the riding you get yourself involved in, the more essential it's gonna be that you're aware of this stuff and have a feel for it.

SURVIVING

With the best will and all the practice in the world, you will sometimes simply fail to avoid a good kicking. So here are some tips on not letting it shorten your surfing career.

How you respond to a wipeout depends on one thing – the consequences. Intimidating though it is to be tumbled out of control, if the wave is under six foot and in deep water you will probably come to no harm as long as you relax everything except your grip on your paddle and wait for the noise to stop before you try to roll. If however your wave is bigger or breaking into shallow water on a nasty sharp coral reef, you may have a bit more cause to worry!

Or, if there is a chance that there is someone inside you that you might crash into while upside yer head! This is where freestyle or hot-dogging skills are useful. Expert kayakers have an almost superhuman ability to land right side up, like a cat, after a negative three-dimensional transient experience. If you have these skills, use 'em. If you don't, learn them! Sooner or later they will save you or someone else from getting red on the wrong side. →

← Sometimes, the beating you are going to get is so severe that you cannot be doing twisty-turny gymnastics and waving your paddle around under water for fear of getting your arms ripped out of their sockets. I'm not joking, shoulder and other joint dislocations are common in this scenario. If it is this bad, tuck up tight with your head on the deck and your paddle along the boat. Hold on tightly to everything, including your breakfast. Empty your mind of thoughts – this will make the air in your lungs last longer (no, really it will...) and may also stop you from suddenly relaxing and uncurling from your relatively safe foetal position in the mistaken belief that you have worked out what is going on!

In my experience there is often a moment when the wave appears to have released you and there are no powerful forces acting on your body. I advise you to be sure of this before you try to become pro-active again. Because sometimes this moment of calm means that you are free-falling down the front of the wave, or possibly surfacing rapidly up the back of it to be recirculated once more. If you are very good at 3-D spatial awareness, you may be able to detect quickly that the worst is over. This would be good, because there is often a wave behind the one that gave you a slapping, it's usually bigger, and you are now in sorry shape! So floating around upside down for longer than necessary isn't going to make it go better the second time – get up and get going!

WARNING

SURF SUBJECT TO UNEXPECTED LIFE-THREATENING WAVES & CURRENTS

CLIMBING ON ROCKS, SWIMMING & WADING UNSAFE

NO

train for kayak surfing. The sport is too new for any correlation to have emerged between the behaviour of riders and their resulting physical condition. Some train their heads off, and are mediocre and injury-prone. Some, like double World Champion Tim Thomas, famously never got in a boat between contests and still managed to destroy the competition without ever succumbing to injury. So, reading this is a complete waste of time, right? Wrong... There are a few things we can say for certain.

A The more time you spend boating, the more skilful you will become. B The more you boat the more tired you will become. C Boating while tired increases the likelihood of injury, and encourages the practice of poor technique which makes you less skilful. Therefore, D you should boat as much as you can without becoming so tired that it impairs performance.

You will find that this isn't as much as you'd like. If there's no-one else out and I can take regular rides, I rarely last more than an hour.

But that doesn't mean I can't go out again after a rest.

Some people say that if you can boat as much as you like, there is no better training, and you need never do anything except paddle. I don't agree. I think kayaking is actually quite bad for you if taken to excess, and that you can't train as much as you might benefit from without risk of injury, particularly spinal problems and tendon-related wrist problems. If you cross-train, out of the boat, you can improve your physical strength and stamina in between kayaking sessions and reverse their negative effects. I favour board-surfing, because it reverses the spinal flexion prevalent in kayakers, and the swimming action strengthens the arms without causing wrist injury. At the same time, you'll certainly learn a lot of things about waves and riding.

That said, many people find that they can't get to the water as much as they'd like - so maybe you want to train without getting in the water, at the gym or at home or by doing another sport. There is a section in this book designed for just such an eventuality.

If you can get to the water and surf a kayak or a board regularly, clearly that is the best thing you could possibly be doing with your time. As long as you don't forget to earn some money or at least eat now and again, and to call your mother. I try to do some kind of kayaking or board sport every day. I regularly fail in this endeavour, and end up doing it about three hundred days per year. Not a bad result – it means I rarely need to cross-train, thus managing to avoid activities like running which have negative effects as well as their undoubted benefits.

REVERT:

01

Here's an example of a basic revert using a fundamental playboating skill. To a freestyle paddler this would be a bandit/cartwheel, but in this instance it's been used as a recovery when the rider has stalled in the whitewash. It's not easy to spin around quickly in a finned kayak once momentum is lost, so the kayaker slices the tail under to make a quick vertical transition, with a view to recovering into continuing the ride in the power zone.

02

Another stolen skateboard move, a REVERT is the name given to any spinning or transitional rotation on a steep face that recovers back into a viable riding position. In this instance the paddler reverts to riding conventionally after a brief foray into the playful world of freestyle!

03

the purpose of moves & tricks
and the difference between them

There are basically two schools of thought when it comes to playing in the surf. One is that there is no 'right' way to surf, and that whatever you enjoy doing is cool. The other is that one should adhere as closely as possible to the more widely accepted forms, and surf 'like everyone else'. People from the two different camps are basically unable to play together without irritating each other.

If you are reading this book, it's probably safe to say that you fall into the latter group. I do, although I'm not averse to being a little experimental if there's no-one around whose day will be adversely affected. But there is a difference of opinion even among us. That difference concerns whether or not any given move or manouevre constitutes an appropriate part of the ride, or is just a trick, and whether such "tricks" enhance or detract from a ride.

Mostly what determines a boater's opinion on this is their background. Freestyle kayakers do tricks that serve no purpose other than that they are aesthetically pleasing and demonstrate their skill. They tend, when they surf, to bring these sort of tricks with them and feel that their rides are enhanced by them. I'm talking about tricks like blunts, donkey-flips (or California rolls as some call them) and soup tricks like cartwheels. Surfers from a non-freestyle background usually don't experiment with these types of tricks and will spend their time developing much more functional techniques which can in some cases become just as radical and demanding.

The same thing happened in the world of board surfing. It used to be all about functional riding and radical manoeuvres reflected that. But surfers from a skateboarding background brought a whole panoply of aerial, ollie and flip-tricks to the game, many of which have since become very popular, highly regarded and in some cases useful.

Of course, the actual ride is not the only place for such things. It's fun to do tricks while paddling out, like the wavewheel, kickflip and macho move. Flatwater cartwheeling, bow and stern stalls, stern squirts and screw-ups can keep us occupied out back as we wait for the next set. Although they're not always popular – the line-up can be a mellow place where people are communing quietly with nature. A kayaker flailing and splashing incessantly may not be a welcome sight.

That aside, the question is whether or not the trick enhances the rider's performance. If it doesn't detract from the length and dynamism of the ride, and it looks cool or clever, then I guess it is cool. But many would disagree. If, on the other hand, the trick actually extends the ride or adds energy to it, then there really is no dispute, it should definitely stay!

RADICAL MOVES

It's tempting to jump straight to this section. We've got the basics, let's just get radical! But surfing, unlike most other freestyle/freeride disciplines, is not all about moves. The wave is not the platform on which you perform – it is your dancing partner. So while you must have an eye for your footwork and not tread on her toes, you should not overly obsess about your own moves, or she'll waltz away from you without a moment's regret. So read on by all means, these fancy steps may come in handy when you catch the eye of a pretty wave one day. But don't forget what I said...

snap, slash & layback

SNAP - a concept stolen from shortboard surfers, and until recently, quite impossible in a kayak. The move towards very short and lightweight surf boats, and the development of the type of skills that deliver the explosive rotation seen in wavewheels and blunts, has brought this kind of power-move within our reach.

A snap is basically a super-quick direction change delivered by pre-rotating the body, sometimes as much as 180° and then whipping the boat around to face the same way. Shortboard surfers pivot around the back foot (which is over the fins) but the kayak will tend to turn around the centre (which is over the fins) unless, and this looks and feels a lot more powerful, you can get all your weight onto an outstretched paddle blade.

This idea of pre-rotating, unweighting the boat and then flicking it around will come easily to anyone who can blunt or cartwheel. If you aren't familiar with that type of thing, just think of it as a very aggressive turn, driven by the paddle through massive shoulder rotation. This is not normally the way I'd suggest making a turn, but if you do it hard enough it works and is very cool.

The difficult thing in a kayak is to make sure the tail comes unstuck and slices through the air not the water. Which is where the whole unweighting thing is important. It's not so different from a tail-slash top turn, but a snap **A** is so much quicker; **B** can be a bottom turn, cutback or anything; **C** doesn't necessarily (or indeed usually) slash the tail across the wave.

In a perfect world you could head vertically up the face and snap the boat towards the break. How great would that be? Let me know if you can do this, I've been trying for ages. This 'vertical power-snap' is the Holy Grail for many stand up surfers, and a constant reminder to kayakers of how much lies ahead of us →

SLASH - Wave-ski surfers do a lot of this. Simply a top turn where the power and aggression of the move causes the fins to slide and the tail of the boat to slash across or through the top of the wave. Leaves a great trail in the wave, so it's a very photogenic manoeuvre...

The slash is similar to yet very different from the snap. In a snap you rotate the boat as much as possible, as fast as possible, using a lot of strong body language delivered through the paddle blade. In a slash you power up your turning moment by loading up the rail more and more while sending your chi running wide of the turn, so that the turn overcomes the grip of rail and fin and sends the tail slashing around. You shouldn't really need to use the paddle much, except for a bit of support and confidence. Some artful fore and aft weight shift can help define the exact moment that the tail slides, but that's very boat dependant so you'll just have to mess around and find out what works for you.

The slash is a superbly quick and flamboyant way of doing a roundhouse cutback, for which there is often less time than you thought...

LAYBACK - actually a stolen skateboard move, but particularly useful in a surf kayak. Skaters use it to un-weight the board so that it will slide or turn more quickly, and because the radical body position looks cool and dynamic. And exactly the same is true for a kayak, especially a finned one.

Use layback variants of the Slash, Revert or Snap to add a radical element to your ride. How is it done? Flatten yourself on the back deck. The layback gets your weight back behind the fins, and can also add momentum to the tail which makes it break away and slide. It takes quite a bit of commitment to try such a radical position, but it does enable you to do some pretty funky things.

You may find that laybacks put a lot of stress on your back or on your abs – it helps enormously if your kayak has really good thigh grips and outfitting (which many surf kayaks don't) or some kind of quad strap system like a wave-ski. A lot of kayakers retro fit these since they aren't usually available from the manufacturer.

Spins are a lot of fun, and can be functional to boot. Some hardcore kayak surfers might disrespect your spins, thinking you should only carve functional turns, but the spin is a fantastic way to stall back into the pocket, and a useful skill to learn as a recovery technique should you lose the tail in a steep section.

If you paddle a playboat or similar flat-bottomed kayak without fins, spins will be very easy. You may have learnt to do them already, perhaps on river waves, or just reacting to the tail sliding away from you down the wave. Even if you have small playboat fins, they won't do much to impede your spins. All you have to do is relax the rail until the tail starts to loosen up, and then go with it, keeping the boat fairly flat. I do recommend pre-rotating your body as much and as early as possible.

If you have bigger fins, like the thruster fin set-up most people use on surf kayaks, you may find it takes a fair bit of effort, using either body language or a shove from the paddle, to get the spin started. After that though, it feels

much the same. Once the fins are cavitating (have air around them instead of water) they don't grip much until they are going forward again. At this point the air gets stripped away by your forward speed and the fins revert to behaving as their maker intended.

With huge fins, like those used by some big-wave surfers, it may be almost impossible to get the fins to release. Almost is the operative word though – if you spin quickly enough with your weight balanced over the fins, you are effectively spinning around the fin and it shouldn't resist too much. Though it is very difficult to perfect this.

Fins also have a chi and charc of their own. Once you are planing, they no longer exist as a fixed point any more, but have acquired forces derived from the water flowing over them, and these forces will resist your attempts to make the fin act like a point frozen in time.

This fin-charc is one reason why I think spinning is a valid endeavour. Because in

addition to the value of flat-spins, elevated spins and reverts as useful repositioning techniques and dynamic moves in their own right, they are the only way I have come across of acquainting yourself with the strange and complex world in which your fins live. Once you have some hull speed, it is as though your fins are riding in grooves, like a slot-car. But those grooves can be bent out of shape by your intent, and it is also possible to introduce cavitation into the equation, making the grooves behave as though they were made of rubber, gripping the fins but also allowing them to turn around. If you have more than one fin it's best not to think about this too hard. Because it works really well as a visualization tool until you overthink it, when you realize it couldn't be like that really.

Sometimes, for no reason I can discern, the boat just slides down the wave despite your best attempts to hold the rail. It can happen in a turn – attempt a radical cutback, and the boat keeps sliding along the wave when you thought it would grip. I do not know why this happens. Maybe it is something to do with air getting under the hull and causing another kind of cavitation. I think I may understand this fully when I have practised enough spinning, so continue to spin I will.

OFFSIDE SPINS - It's one thing to spin with the natural shape of the wave – turning up-wave (say, clockwise if you're riding right) – but quite another to spin back towards the pocket. To a river boater, doing this might be thought of as a roundhouse or blunt, and it is very hard to do in the surf unless indeed you use a blunt-like weight-throw to unstick the tail. Body-boarders are particularly good at offside spins and will be impressed if you can do them well in your kayak, even if no one else is... They tend to do them ad-hoc especially if they are riding out onto the shoulder and need to lose speed and height. In a kayak you don't tend to shed height as the offside spin is sticky, and if anything takes you up-wave, so it's usually best to try it as part of a roundhouse cutback – setting up for the spin once the boat is riding towards the pocket.

01

02

03

04

05

06

PICTURED LEFT -
It is one thing to pull off a 360 spin - quite another to perform it while riding along in the pocket without interrupting the ride. The secret is to have a good feel for the wave and to keep your intent focussed on your chosen charc.

PICTURED ABOVE -
Initiating the move from a shoulder ride relies on having the weight off the tail and balanced over the fins, as can be seen here. Bill loads up the blade to launch a spin.

tube ride or 'getting shacked'

's everyone's classic image of surfing and an awesome experience, whether you are sitting, standing, or lying down. Never easy to achieve and fraught with problems in a kayak.

What we are talking about here is riding in the hollow part of the wave when the lip is coming right over and forming a 'tube' inside which it is still possible to surf, albeit at a very extreme and committed angle – usually you need to be breaking directly across the face of the wave.

Not all waves do this. Waves that do are not exactly the Holy Grail of surfing, since they are found in many spots all over the world, but it is certainly a minority of rideable waves that actually tube.

The terminology of this type of riding is ambiguous. Surfers talk of being tubed, barrelled, covered up. To some all of these expressions are generalizations, referring to any ride where the surfer is inside the tube of a barrelling wave. But to many, each has a subtly different meaning – a tube ride finishing with the rider escaping out of the end of the tube, a barrel implying a closed end, the rider not escaping or escaping by punching out through the curtain of falling water. Cover-ups usually refer to the lip pitching over the rider's head, but not entirely enclosing him to form a tube. And some will talk of 'getting shacked' or a multitude of other colloquialisms for the ultimate surfing experience.

Sooner or later, if you ride as deep as possible in the pocket in hollow, barrelling waves, you will get the opportunity to get covered up or completely tubed. All well and good. You will probably not be so deep though because the section ahead of you will be pitching hard, you'll have charged ahead to try to make it. If you don't, the lip may throw over your head and you'll be overturned by the white water. Kayakers tend to lack the acceleration to stall deep into the pocket and then accelerate away fast enough to keep up with a tubing wave.

The other problem is that in a barrelling section the water is going up the front of the wave at a colossal rate. You might at times need to ride almost straight down the wave in order to stay on the face and avoid being sucked over the falls. But doing that precludes riding across the face and hence making the section. Shortboarders can handle this because they can make instant direction changes, and have superb acceleration due to the shortness of the board and their ability to weight shift. Body boarders do well too, since they are fast and can sideslip on the wave to maintain position. Kayakers will struggle in this domain. But it is not impossible. Practise, a lot, somewhere reasonably safe (barrelling waves are unfortunately found usually in shallow water), and you will get tube rides. And perhaps their rarity will make them all the more special.

■ PICTURED ABOVE & INSET -
The tube becomes a barrel.
Realising that there will be no
escaping the end of this heavy
tube, Nathan turns to ride out
in the last possible window of
opportunity. Busting out through
the curtain can be fun, but not in
waves like these...

aerial

TIPS:

Being able to do a really good bottom turn into OTL sequence in your own time is essential, and gives you the head-space to look out for opportunity. Speaking of opportunity - look out for wedges. If you can drive up to the lip so that you hit the top of a wedge at the same time or slightly before you hit the lip, you will really fly.

Well, I don't know what the fuss is about. An aerial is just a super-late top turn, where you forget to make the turn until you've ridden right through the lip into the sky!

All joking aside, you don't see proper kayak aerials very often. This is because there are very few riders, or boats, or combinations of the two, who can ride aggressively enough in the kind of steep wave conditions that make aerials possible. Doesn't stop us trying though; and here's how: o——

(Believe it or not point six is the most important one. You'll feel a lot more comfortable with all this if you're good at wavewheels and kickflips pp124-126)

No1 Master your bottom turns and 'off the lip' top turns until you are very comfortable performing them.

No2 Do a good, fast bottom turn and hold the edge a little longer than usual; angle up the wave with lots of speed toward a steep section, then use your knees to drop your down-wave rail. If the hull ends up flat to the wave's surface, that's perfect.

No3 Stay forward, and reach forward with your down-wave hand as your nose reaches the lip of the wave. Don't pre-rotate the way you normally do though.

No4 Do a powerful stroke at the last moment as the boat begins to rise into the air. Take the stroke all the way back. As well as helping the launch this will take your weight all the way back, and pre-rotate you for the turn in the air.

No5 Lean onto your lower rail, while still keeping your weight above the boat, to aim the nose of your boat back down at the wave.

No6 Do not try to make the turn in the air!

No7 Lean forward and allow yourself to consider the turn. With luck you'll land tail first, but if you don't it's good you're leaning forward isn't it?

No8 Ride down the wave and get ready to bottom turn. Try to look bored.

paddle out tricks

Here are some tricks you can do as you paddle out over waves. They may not be riding techniques per se, but they do teach you a couple of things that are difficult to learn on the face of the wave. And, they are fun and cool.

WAVEWHEEL -

a flat water cartwheel (double-ender, really) which is performed utilizing the wave-face as a kind of launch ramp to get the nose of the boat high enough in the air that you can then smash it into the water to start the cartwheel. If you are familiar with the principles of cartwheeling, especially flat water cartwheels, then this will all be completely straightforward to you. If you've never done anything like that, fear not – it's not as hard as it looks.

A Paddle up the face of a wave that is close to breaking. Once the top starts to break and fall, it's too late. But it needs to be close to breaking, so that it comes to a point at the top rather than being a rounded hump still.

B Accelerate as you go up the face. A lot of people make the mistake of getting up to speed on the flat, and then are unable to sustain the speed up the wave.

C Make your last stroke right in the crest of the wave and launch the boat forward by throwing your weight back. This is called a rocket move, incidentally. As you do this, start to roll the boat onto its side and commit your weight to the blade.

D As the stroke comes to an end and the boat launches into the air, quickly reverse the stroke (drive the blade forward/downward) and hurl the nose of the boat down with your legs. It should

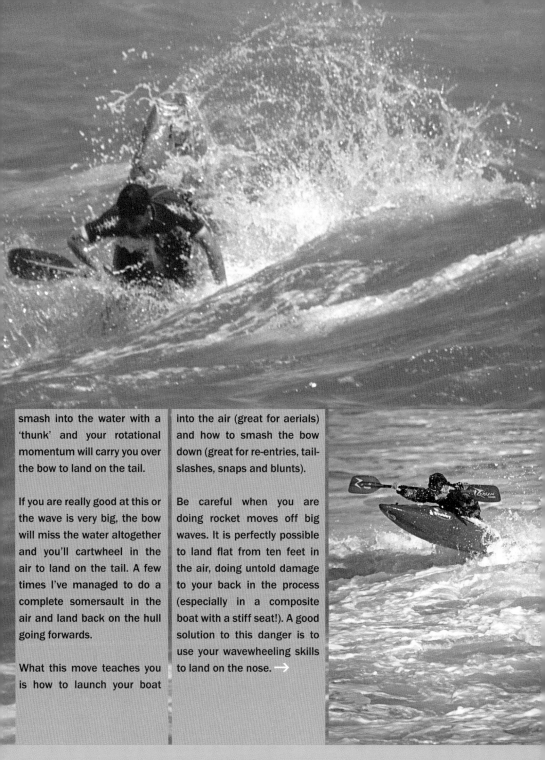

smash into the water with a 'thunk' and your rotational momentum will carry you over the bow to land on the tail.

If you are really good at this or the wave is very big, the bow will miss the water altogether and you'll cartwheel in the air to land on the tail. A few times I've managed to do a complete somersault in the air and land back on the hull going forwards.

What this move teaches you is how to launch your boat into the air (great for aerials) and how to smash the bow down (great for re-entries, tail-slashes, snaps and blunts).

Be careful when you are doing rocket moves off big waves. It is perfectly possible to land flat from ten feet in the air, doing untold damage to your back in the process (especially in a composite boat with a stiff seat!). A good solution to this danger is to use your wavewheeling skills to land on the nose. →

KICKFLIP - another move borrowed from skateboarders. The trick is to flip/rotate your boat/board 360° in the roll plane, in the air – in a boat it's just like an airborne roll.

The kickflip is super-cool if you can do it properly in the air and land flat on the hull without getting your head wet. Most people do feeble ones that are just rolls really. The worst scenario is to do it half-well, because this can put too much strain on your shoulder and risks the classic anterior dislocation all kayakers fear.

■ You'll need a really good rocket move. Which is about powerful body language, but also practising until you're very good at picking when and where to hit the wave. Practise the rocket move, not the whole kickflip. Only once you can launch a massive rocket move every time is it safe to try to flip. Otherwise you'll land on your shoulder too many times, and there'll be tears before bedtime.

■ Next you need your wave-wheel skills. Roll your weight onto the blade at the end of your launch stroke, and do a little bit of the wavewheel smash stroke – not too hard, just enough to bring the nose down ('cos as you rocket it will be pointing up, won't it?). As you do this, keep throwing your weight until you're completely upside down and leaning back. Finally whip the paddle around into a reverse screw-roll position (see pic) and finish the roll with a hip-flick just as you would if you were under water.

■ If you've pulled the nose down enough at the start you'll raise the tail until the boat's parallel with the back of the wave, giving yourself a lot of room to get under it. This is like the ollie at the start of the kickflip on a skateboard.

■ If by some miracle you clean a great flip, sitting up suddenly at the end will pull the nose back up for a bang-flat landing, which is just the icing on the cake.

■ Don't actually use your paddle to try to roll up, especially if the move has gone wrong. Let yourself crash into the water, wait, curse, and roll. Trying to roll as you crash down is what can hurt your shoulder. I can only do a few kickflips a day without my shoulders starting to ache and complain big-time.

blunt & barrel roll

Freestyle enthusiasts may realize that wavewheels have a lot in common with blunts, and kickflips with barrel rolls. You may wonder then, why I have written about them in this order. Well, I think that paddle out tricks belong together, and wave face tricks belong together also. Furthermore, I think learning to wavewheel leads naturally into the kickflip, and that these skills equip us admirably to interpret the moves dealt with on this spread.

BLUNT - an elevated 180° direction change towards the breaking part of the wave. That is the official definition in the world of white water kayak freestyle, so it's not really negotiable. However, I think it's worth mentioning its origins, which are in surfing.

Before the kayak blunt came the roundhouse, a very quick 180° direction change towards the break in imitation of a very snappy roundhouse cutback. The best way to do this on a river wave turned out to be a big weight throw to unload the tail and pivot around the front part of the boat. So as people got better at it and kayak design evolved a bit, the move became more and more elevated until it was really a vertical move, bouncing over and around on the nose, and not a turn at all. That is called a blunt, because it looks a bit like a skateboard trick of the same name.

In a surf kayak the move has to be done a little differently, because you can't generate as much bounce with a weight shift as you can in a playboat. The surf kayak needs some kind of launch ramp, like a wedging wave or a little chop, or a take-off from the lip. So the move relies on some carving speed and the use of the wave's shape to make it happen. But once you sort out the take-off the principle is much the same.

If you do a past vertical blunt that is massively over-rotated (in that it has some roll element) but still basically land backsurfing, that is called by some a 'Pan-Am'. And if you take this move to the extreme, by emphasising the roll aspect and reducing your commitment to the smash as you do in a kickflip, it is easy to see how it can become an aerial 360° barrel roll without the 180° direction change in the yaw plane. The difference between these moves is in some ways only a matter of degree in roll, pitch and yaw.

The ultimate extension of these types of moves would of course be a move which rotates 360° in all three planes. Not commonly done as yet, but something to aspire to! The closest kayakers get at the time of writing is the helix. A helix is a 360° in the yaw plane combined with a 360° in the roll plane at the same time. It is commonly done on river waves with the aid of some massive butt-bouncing air, and can be done the same way in the surf if you are paddling a playboat. But to do it in a surf kayak requires some awesome commitment to a carved aerial charc, in order to achieve the height needed at the same time as enough rotational momentum.

chi (ki)

I don't want impose my personal brand of mysticism on you. But if you want to excel at surfing, you probably have more than a grain of soul. So perhaps you'll be receptive to this idea...

Chi, or ki, is the quasi-alchemical agent which connects you to the invisible world in order that your intent be made manifest in the physical world.

Chi is an oriental mystical concept that, like many, doesn't translate very well. Basically it refers to the energy of your life force, and is very much entangled with the Taoist idea that you must go with the flow in order to succeed. Which is an idea which tends to be very acceptable to kayakers, but less so to those who are accustomed to fighting for every last inch. You can't fight Nature. Well, you can, but you'll lose horribly every time.

This philosophy of following the natural flow of events in your life will, if practised daily, develop in you an enhanced energy, awareness and flow. It will take time, but

harnessing mind, breath and chi will ultimately lend the practitioner a superhuman level of personal power, highly effective for all kinds of things but most especially for surfing. You can't rush the chi-cultivation process – it's like a river, or the ocean. All you can do is prepare, and wait. When it does come, though, it will be implacable. Neither you nor anyone else will be able to stop it, you will become more or less invincible.

The chi style of surfing utilises the wave's speed and energy rather than your own. It is a very sophisticated way of getting the job done while appearing to do very little. When you find yourself

吾不知
其名
強字之
曰道

I CALL IT TAO

MUST HAVE A WORD FOR IT

ITS NAME, IF I

I DO NOT KNOW

needing to hit a move hard, your chi will be manifest in your momentum, potential and kinetic energies going into it, rather than attempting to deliver the power with your own puny physical form. This is what is known in Eastern martial arts as a soft approach, but it doesn't look or feel soft, and its application isn't limited to soft breaks/targets either. In fact it isn't limited to or by anything at all, except the amount of chi you have developed. And a combination of your realism and self-belief, which amounts to the same thing.

If you need to see the world through mechanistic or rational filters, you may feel uncomfortable with this pseudo-spiritual mumbo-jumbo. But bear with me, and if you must you can think of it as a practical technique. Where you look is where you will go, that's how we're wired up. As a kayaker you must already be aware of this. So if you like, you can think of it as looking always to the end point of the next move, or the next but one point of inflection on your chosen charc. I think of it as projecting my spirit (or my chi) along the wave ahead of me, willing it to blend with the pattern of energy in the real world, and simply allowing my physical form to follow that path. You must be at peace with Nature though, or she'll give you a slap.

Conscious thought is a bit of a chi blocker until you become a master. Ultimately you will find that you can think and plan without interfering with your own charc, but at first it's best to empty your mind. This will give your riding a natural realism which both looks and feels good. There are sequences that flow naturally together, and some that don't. Your chi will sort this out for you. Trying to think about it in an attempt to be more radical is a recipe for stepping outside of what is possible for you, and what is pretty. Let your chi take care of it, and don't forget to breathe.

charc the charging or changing arc

It's a term that I have borrowed from squirt boating. It was coined by the master squirt boater and a favourite author of mine, Jim Snyder. He also penned what is, at the time of writing, my favourite quotation, "*Be bold enough to be small enough to let the world be awesome, and it will*".

But we're not talking about that. We're discussing charc. Charc is short for 'charging arc'. It is an especially relevant and important concept to squirt boaters in their quest for mastery of the fluid realm – they use it to describe the ever changing angle of attack of the kayak as the boater reacts to local events and constantly evolves his or her strategy. As Snyder himself wrote, "*Charc can be seen as a tube moving through a series of windows of opportunity. The object of the game is to 'see' the tube, then fit yourself and your boat through it*". The first time I read that, I knew that it was to be even more important to my surfing than it is to my squirt boat paddling.

In using the charc concept, I've come to focus on the 'arc' rather more than the charging. Charging is good, whether you're charging a gnarly section or charging up your potential energy for a drop. But surfing is all about linking arcs of motion whose loci are defined by your rails and your weight throw. And those arcs are constantly evolving as the future wave plays out its grand plan ahead of you. So for us, the charc is an ever 'changing arc'. It is also, in a way, the locus of our chi – the chi-arc!

Some kayakers map out the ride in their mind as a series of contact points. Therein exists an intention, at least, sequentially to hit a series of specific points on the wave in the not too distant future. Conceptually this is not dissimilar to charc or tubism, but it is a little crude, borrowed as it is from the philosophy of river boating where the features are (fairly) static in both space and time. The ocean wave is static in neither, so even your closest contact point does not exist in the physical world until you hit it. And maybe not even then! So not only must you plan to hit points that you can only imagine as yet, but your plan must evolve continuously as you constantly turn out to be wrong. And anyway, an arc is a more natural, fluid and beautiful thing than anything less than an infinite number of points.

TRAINING&FITNESS

As with any sport, the fitter you are the better you will perform, and the less injury prone you will be. That's a given. Kayak surfing is a pretty unusual sport though. You don't need to be super fit and powerful to do it. If you are skilful and chi-ful enough, you can surf with very little exertion. So it's really up to you to decide how important it is to bring more physical strength and endurance to your riding.

That said, kayak surfing can place ludicrous demands on your body. The forces exerted on your frame as you charge a bottom turn or slam in a rail for a snap cutback far exceed anything you could apply with your own strength, because so much momentum and wave energy are amping the power of the move. So if you aren't in good physical mettle when you go out, you're going to be in sorry shape for the journey home.

In order to minimize the risk of injury, it's a good idea to keep yourself flexible, and to make sure you are warmed through and have good mobility before you venture into the water. The next few pages may be helpful in that they show a range of techniques that I have found helpful in physically preparing to go out in the surf.

training for surf kayaking

Waves can beat a kayaker up pretty **bad**. Even 2 foot surf can give you a **right** old kicking. Cartwheeling out **of co**ntrol like a rag doll or being launched at 20mph into hard green water can place significant physical stress on your body. So how are we going to deal? Easy.

First of all, we are going to reduce the likelihood of such an occurrence, to try to ensure that the number of them is kept to a minimum. We are all going to get hammered sometimes, but it stands to reason that the boater who gets hammered once or twice a session is less likely to get hurt than one who gets it every few minutes. So read all the other pages in this book, in particular the bit called 'Surviving', and be good at avoiding disaster.

The next thing to address is making sure we are physically good at paddling around in the surf. If you can paddle fast and for an appropriate amount of time, and have the right physique for jumping or punching waves, it's gotta help, right? I seem to get way more kickings when I'm paddling out, or get caught by a sneaker set, than I do when actually riding. On fairly soft beach-breaks, at any rate.

This is all about training in complimentary ways. Training in the kayak can be very good, but as I've mentioned elsewhere it is also good to cross-train, because paddling alone can be bad for your physique, in particular your spine.

Paddling your surf kayak hard on flat water for five minutes at a time is good. Five minutes on, five minutes rest, repeat ten times. If you train in a different kayak, try to emulate the stroke rate and the amount of paddle pressure that you use in the surf kayak. Once per session, paddle non-stop for twenty minutes at the highest level of effort you can sustain constantly throughout.

If you swim or paddle a surfboard or paddleboard for training, it helps to use hand paddles or webbed gloves. This increases the surface area of your hands and makes it feel more like using a paddle blade.

'Pressure management' techniques like these ensure that you develop the correct size and speed of muscles for paddling. There is no point in developing endurance, since you're not

going to paddle through waves constantly for hours. Equally, a bodybuilder might be much stronger than you are, but still wouldn't be able to sprint faster to get around a section, or huck a kickflip for that matter!

That takes care of paddling – now for wave jumping. Well, this is all about abs and quads. Abdominal muscles are the ones that make up your six-pack, and quadriceps are the big muscles in your thighs. Thighs? Yup, believe it or not, your thigh muscles do more than half the work of moving your upper body around in a kayak.

ABS – train these by doing crunches and leg lifts. Crunches are better for you than sit-ups. But don't do thousands of them. Do them in short sets, maybe twenty at a time. When this becomes ludicrously easy, start doing them while holding a weight under your chin. Start with a small weight. And if you ever build up to doing them with a 10kg weight, it might be wise to leave it at that. Do crunches three days a week, not every day. How many sets of twenty you do on a crunch day can depend on your lifestyle and how flat/blown out the surf is. Leg lifts are an isometric exercise which train your abs to maintain your posture when a wave tries to knock you out of shape. Hold the position for ten seconds at a time. Don't overdo it as they can exacerbate back problems that kayakers are quite prone to.

QUADS – these also need training in both dynamic and isometric modes. The best dynamic exercises are squats or squat-thrusts, step exercises (or running upstairs) and sit-ups with your feet under the sofa (not very good for your back though). A good isometric one is to maintain a chair-sitting position with your back against a wall, but with no chair. Hold this for a minute at a time.

These exercises should help you to paddle your kayak quickly and efficiently, and reduce as much as possible the number of times you get caught inside or fail to make it through a wave. But to make sure you are fit for the inevitable instances when all of the above comes to naught... read on.

preparation warming up and down, stretching, and stuff like that...

You should always ensure that your body is warmed up before any kind of strenuous activity. This prepares you for sudden exertion and minimizes the risk of injury. Once it is warmed through your body will be much more flexible and able to accommodate shocks, impact and over extension. Even stretching should not be attempted until you are warmed up.

There are two aspects to warm-ups. The first is to get your heart going a bit faster than the normal resting rate, so that your cardiovascular system is getting the heat and oxygen everywhere it needs to be in preparation for exercise. The second is to limber up the muscles. So it's best to get everything moving if you can.

Most athletes like to formulate a routine that prepares them mentally as well as physically for activity. In this sense, it is best to use the same warm-up activity every time. However, if you surf every day, this can get boring and it might be better to vary the warm-up.

The best way to warm is with gentle exercise. Walking briskly, or running gently, swimming if the water is warm, or playing Frisbee on the beach – all great ways to get yourself warmed up. Driving to the break with the heated seats on and the air-con turned up hot does not count as a warm-up!

Stretching is a controversial preparation. Until recently, trainers have recommended going from the warm-up into a stretch programme, but now many theorize that it is better to go straight into activity but gently at first, in order to stretch naturally and in the right way. All well and good, but you might get back-looped by a wave within thirty seconds of getting afloat. So I think where kayak surfing is concerned, a compromise may be worthwhile. I like to stretch a little out of the boat, then stretch in the boat to ensure full mobility and that everything can move around as it should. I also try to re-stretch once I am out the back for the first time, and although this sometimes has hilarious consequences in my fairly unstable kayak, I usually find that my mobility has improved dramatically after the paddle-out.

competition

Like any sport, kayak surfing has it's competitive angle. It is human nature that any group of enthusiasts together will devise a set of rules to determine who is the best. Personally, I am more of a soul surfer than a competition afficionado, but there is no doubt that it is a fast-track way to get your surfing in sync with other riders. If you don't ride in the generally accepted way, you won't score any points. There's nothing like it for getting you up to speed. And competition has a marvellous way of shattering any delusions you may have about how good you are! Judging a freestyle/ freeride sport like surfing is an inevitably flawed procedure, but over the years competition enthusiasts have evolved a set of criteria that seems to come up with the right result.

HOW A COMPETITION IS JUDGED

The format of competition may well change, but it's probably safe to say that the basics will endure. At the time of writing, kayak surfing is judged on 'length and quality of ride'. The longer the ride, the more points you score. The longer you stay in the critical position in the power-pocket and the more dynamic the moves you use to achieve this, the better your score will be. Nowadays, events are often judged by professional board-surfing judges, and so riding in the style of a short-boarder does tend to score higher.

Usually, the event will be made up of twenty-minute heats for four people, and the best three wave scores you achieve during the heat will be added together to give your result. The two highest scoring paddlers in the heat advance to the next round, until the field is whittled down to a final four.

What often comes as a surprise to new competitors (especially if they are already expert kayakers or perhaps have experience of freestyle

boating) is that you don't tend to get any points in a surf contest for moves which are not functional. It's not about doing tricks on the wave, it's about riding as deep as possible in the critical part. But the more spectacular the functional techniques you use to continue and complete the ride, the better your surfing is deemed to be.

The up-side of competition is, as I have said, the reality injection it inevitably gives you. If you aren't getting such long, dynamic and stylish rides as your fellow competitors, you will know about it. The down-side is that it can hamper innovation. The judges are, at the time of writing, unlikely to reward your space-Godzilla take-off,

or to give you extra points for a cross-bow top turn. Neither are points awarded for paddle out tricks like kickflips and wavewheels, despite these being the tricks most greatly admired by many who boat in the surf. But I think that's OK. We can take what competition has to offer us and learn from it, keeping in mind that what it offers us isn't everything.

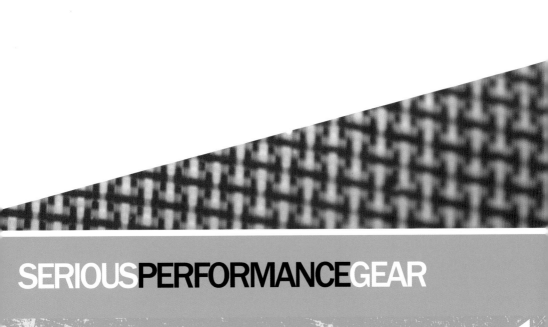

SERIOUSPERFORMANCEGEAR

boats

There are many different kinds of craft that you can use in the surf, some of which are described at the beginning of the book. But those that can truly be called surf kayaks are a much more limited selection. There are a lot of different designs on the market, but they are all pretty similar, and it takes a lot of experience (or a lot of paddling demo boats) to be able easily to identify the differences in their characteristics.

FREESTYLE KAYAKS THAT ARE GOOD IN THE SURF

Boats like this are great fun in the surf. The best ones are over 2.2m long and have no significant rocker breaks. Some come with fin-boxes as standard, but many kayakers modify their kayaks by adding fin-boxes, or bolt-thru wakeboard fins.

FAIRLY SYMMETRICAL SURF KAYAKS

Some surf kayaks are designed to be of fairly balanced volume in order to make them feel more like playboats. These boats are easier to control and to paddle around in, and although the surfing performance may be slightly compromised, these boats feel more natural to anyone who has come from a white water kayaking background. They often utilize a sitting position very similar to that of a freestyle kayak, but feature a hull and rail design with fin-boxes that is purely surf-orientated.

☐ Unlike plastic playboats, most surf kayaks have the minimum of outfitting. If you wish to add a lap belt or thigh straps such as these you will have to retro-fit them yourself. Not too difficult and a great advantage for radical moves. Note the quick-release cord at the attachment point.

"SURF MACHINES WITHOUT COMPROMISE, HAVING A HULL SIMILAR TO A SURFBOARD, FINS, AND A SITTING POSITION THAT KEEPS THE KNEES INBOARD"

LOW TAIL SURF KAYAKS □————————————————□

These boats are surf machines without compromise, having a hull similar to a surfboard, fins, and a sitting position that keeps the knees inboard to reduce drag in the wave face. Unfortunately performance like this comes at a price – the knees together position is alien to anyone used to a white water kayak, and the short, low tail makes the boat unbalanced both to paddle and to control in a wipeout. Many of these boats also have narrow hulls and hence are quite unstable until they are planing. However, they are fast, turn from further back like a ski or board, and are the weapon of choice for most people who are serious about their kayak surfing.

gear & clothing

things you should consider when choosing soft-wear for kayak surfing

SPRAYDECKS – your spraydeck (some call 'em spray skirts) must keep water out well enough that you don't start to lose performance and have to go in and empty. Good ones will keep the boat completely dry inside.

It should go without saying that your deck should never blow off or implode no matter how heavy the surf. If your boat has a fibreglass cockpit rim, you don't need a very tough deck since even a basic neoprene deck will stay on. On a plastic kayak, however, you need a really high-performance spraydeck. This doesn't mean one with lots of Kevlar and reinforcing on – these decks are quite stiff and actually more likely to blow than a stretchier one. A good test is to put the deck on the boat, then pick up the whole lot holding only the spraydeck, and swing it around. If the deck starts to come off, it's not good enough.

Much overlooked. Some boats are pretty tight on footroom but most allow you to wear something on your feet. If you only ever surf sandy beach-breaks, maybe socks will be enough for you. If you might need to clamber on wet rocks, it's a different matter. Here's a short list of ways I have hurt my feet a lot while kayak surfing:

- Getting out of boat onto sharp coral reef
- Climbing down cliffs to get to water
- Clambering over barnacle covered rocks
- Being stung by poisonous fish while walking in sandy shallows
- Trying to kick the boat off while getting ashore in shallow water
- Rubbing the skin off on the inside of composite boat
- Crushing the toes when the nose of the boat hit bottom in a loop.

STAYING WARM AND/OR DRY - depends on the climate, obviously. What you wear on your legs is fairly immaterial because they're going to be in the boat... but what you wear on your upper body has to keep water from going inside the spraydeck tube. You could wear a white water-style cag, with or without thermals, or a thin neoprene rash-vest style item. Or in very cold water, a wetsuit with some rash vest over the top to seal the deck tube. Wetsuits tend to restrict the arm muscles too much for kayaking though.

SAFETY - some people wear buoyancy aids and helmets, some don't. If you are in any doubt I suggest you wear safety equipment. There are different schools of thought about this, as you can see from the pictures throughout this book..

So, I hope you can see now why some sort of shoes are in order. You might think that I would have learnt this after only one or two incidents, but at least you can learn from my foolhardy attempts to economize.

fins & paddles

It might seem odd to discuss these two things together, but in a way they do the same job. Once you are planing, anyway.

PADDLES - a friend of mine once suggested that where kayak surfing is concerned you might as well paddle with two sponges on a stick. He was of course exaggerating but the sheer lack of flat water performance of a surf kayak does make hi-tech paddles a little redundant. Anything that feels nice to hold and to paddle with will probably do the job. It can be problematic to use paddles that are too long. I am 183cms tall and use a 182cm paddle.

FINS - without fins, you sideslip down the wave, lack forward speed, and run wide on every turn. At best you fail to make precise dynamic progress, and at worst you simply spin out of control. The solution is the black art of fins. No one seems to understand them, and I'm no exception. History has shown that the following configurations work well though.

■ Tri-fin Thruster - the most common set-up for both surfboards and kayaks. The outer fins (thrusters) are foiled like an aircraft wing so that they generate lift up the wave, and they work in conjunction with the centre fin to accelerate the flow and drive the boat through turns (venturi effect). The centre fin should be one fin's width further back than the thrusters,

and the whole set-up should be positioned so that you can get your weight over the fins, or in front of them. Putting them further forward gives an easy-turning, twitchy feel, but slower. Putting them too far back makes the boat fast but nearly impossible to turn.

■ Single-fin - gives you the lateral grip of the tri-fin but no extra drive through turns. It's usually bigger to make the surface area up to that of three smaller ones. Because it's in the centre it can come out of the water when you lean.

■ Twin-fin - a very unstable set-up but popular with some. Gives a lot less grip than a tri-fin or single-fin, and a very twitchy feel.

■ Quad-fin - two fins each side quite close together. Working on the principle that you only use one side of the boat at a time, this system allows the two working fins to be closer together than a tri-fin format, which may make them work together better.

Basically you just have to try all these things, see how you go. Clearly, bigger fins give you more grip and more drive, but also more drag. Also, if you go really big you can only turn the boat at its natural carving radius – no amount of muscle will overcome the grip of the fins. Really long fins make it impossible to beach launch.

■ Fins on a surfboard are at the back. The reason fins on a surf kayak are not, is because your centre of gravity is further forward. Remember, you need to be able to get your weight over the fins when you lean back, and in front of them when you lean forward. This is equally true of a stand up surfer... it's just that they can shift their weight a lot further!

≫ EPILOGUE

This is where I leave you. Kayak surfing is in its infancy. It has only just found its direction and started to be cool in the eyes of more than just the lunatic fringe. In recent years kayakers have begun to be accepted at hot, critical breaks all over the planet. In 2003 kayakers surfed successfully at Teahupo'o, the undisputed most hardcore wave in the eyes of surfers the world over. In doing these things, the best kayak surfers around are finding their place in the world of surfing, as well as discovering their limitations and those of their genre.

I have no doubt that there is much craziness to come. Kayakers (myself included) are trying to push the boundaries and pull off the latest surfboard moves, towing into ever more implausible wave faces, and travelling to ever more remote regions in search of adventure. This is the end, but it's only the beginning...

Bill x

PDV 969G

glossary selected terms briefly explained

A-FRAME - The name surfers give to a wave whose face slopes down equally both sides, meaning that you could take off at the apex and get a progressive shoulder ride either way.

AIR BLADE - The paddle blade that is not currently in the water.

BARRELLING - When the lip of a wave curls right over and encloses a tube of air inside the wave.

BERNOULLI EFFECT - The effect of fluid flowing past a wing shaped object like a fin or paddle, exerting a powerful force in the direction of the convex face.

CHI & CHARC - See pp130-133.

CAUGHT INSIDE - Trapped inshore by the breaking waves - see Inside and Deep.

CRITICAL - can mean risky or dangerous but is more often used to describe a position very close to or under the breaking part of the wave.

FOAM-BALL - a soft and rounded broken section that it may be possible to ride around.

INFLECTION - A variation on a curve or alignment. A point of inflection is a change in rate or direction of curvature.

INSIDE - the area (usually) found inshore of the line-up where the waves are breaking, or the area closer to the peak than most of the line-up - see Deep.

MACKING - Derived from the American Mack truck. Anything that carries a lot of momentum, such as extra-powerful waves.

OUTSIDE - The area (usually) found offshore of the line-up. A call of "outside!" usually means a big set is coming.

PEAK - The high point along the face of a wave, which is presumed to be the point from which it will start breaking.

DEEP - can mean depth of water but more often means an inside or critical position. 'Sitting deep' means waiting nearer or further into the breaking section than the rest of the line-up.

DIFFRACTION - Change in the directions and intensities of waves after passing by or over an obstacle or through an aperture.

PILE - Also called whitewash, foam. The white aerated part of the broken wave.

POCKET - The most hollow part of the green wave right next to the breaking/broken section.

PURLING - Burying or snagging the bow of the boat under water, usually by accident.

SECTION - The parts that the length (or life) of a wave face can be subdivided into according to the different ways in which they break.

SET - Waves tend to come in groups with flat spells in between, and the group is called a set. Sometimes waves will come all the time, but occasionally a larger set will come through. Set waves are normally about 1.4 x the size of the norm, and they often come in threes, although the vagaries of interference between different swell systems can generate sets of any number of waves.

SHOALING - The reducing of the depth of water in one area.

SHOULDER - Some kayakers refer to the shoulder as the breaking bit of the wave you ride next to. It is more commonly used by surfers to describe the green part of a wave too far from the pocket that drops off and cannot provide a good ride. To many kayakers a 'shoulder ride' is a good thing, but surfers might use it to describe a poor, non-critical ride. It's important to note that they are talking about different things!

SOUP - The area inside, where the waves are all broken.

SWELL PERIOD - The elapsed time (seconds) between successive waves in a deep-water swell passing a fixed point. The longer the period the better quality and higher energy the waves will tend to be. The actual break will not exhibit as long a time between waves as the quoted deep-water period.

VENTURI EFFECT - The effect of fluid being forced through a bottle-neck shaped structure (like between two fins). The result is a dramatic acceleration of the flow rate and this can make the boat accelerate.

■ **PICTURED** - Nathan Eades fires his Marauder under a Teahupo'o lip. The colossal speed has the boat riding only on the tiny tail-part of the hull.

acknowledgements

All photographs taken by and copyright of Helen Metcalfe except:

4-5 goatboater.com

6-7 background Bill Mattos

12 shortboarder and bodyboard goatboater.com

18-19 goatboater.com except C Duncan Eades

20 F goatboater.com

22 Duncan Eades

24-25 goatboater.com

29 goatboater.com

30 Oskar Martinez

36 goatboater.com

40-41, 42 goatboater.com

52, 55 Oskar Martinez

70-71 goatboater.com

79 goatboater.com

80-81 main goatboater.com

88-89 Oskar Martinez

92-93 main goatboater.com

93 inset, Duncan Eades

97-103 goatboater.com

109 Steve Childs

118-119 goatboater.com

120-121 Duncan Eades

123 Oskar Martinez

134-139 goatboater.com

141 top & bottom right goatboater.com

centre inset Oskar Martinez

143 Oskar Martinez

151-153 goatboater.com

154-155 top goatboater.com

suggested reading

'The Crystal Ball' (p73) first appeared in Canoe & Kayak UK in September 2003.

Kayak Rolling, Loel Collins, Pesda Press, 2004

Satellite image (p75), copyright NERC Satellite Receiving Station, University of Dundee.

Practical Guide to Kayaking and Canoeing, Bill Mattos, Lorenz Books, 2002

Quotation (p133) from 'The Squirt Book', Jim Snyder, Globe Pequot Press, 1997.

Squirt Boating and Beyond, Jim Snyder, Menasha Ridge Press, 2001

To see what else is available from Pesda Press...
visit our website.

www.pesdapress.com